DANIEL PLOOF

ATTRIBUTES
OF A
Godly Marriage

FROM: "I DO" TO: "I WILL!"

GALLATIN, TENNESSEE

Attributes of a Godly Marriage: From "I Do" to "I Will!"
Copyright © 2025 by Daniel Ploof

Psalm51 PUBLISHING

All Rights Reserved. No part of this publication may be reproduced, distributed, or transmitted in any form or by any means, including photocopying, recording, or other electronic or mechanical methods, without the prior written permission of the publisher, except as permitted by U.S. copyright law.

Library of Congress Control Number: 2025920329

ISBN: 978-1-966758-03-7 (print)
ISBN: 978-1-966758-04-4 (e-book)

Scripture quotations are from the ESV® Bible (The Holy Bible, English Standard Version®), © 2001 by Crossway, a publishing ministry of Good News Publishers. Used by permission. All rights reserved.

Cover Image: freepik.com
Book Editor: Amber Ploof

CONTENTS

	Preface	5
	Introduction	7
	Prologue	9
Day 1	DEVOTION: *I will love you with all my heart.*	13
Day 2	COMMITMENT: *I will never leave or forsake you.*	15
Day 3	SECURITY: *I will guard and protect you.*	17
Day 4	PROVISION: *I will provide for our family's needs.*	19
Day 5	BURDENS: *I will carry you when you are weary.*	21
Day 6	GENTLENESS: *I will shepherd your heart.*	23
Day 7	SELF-CONTROL: *I will pursue godliness daily.*	25
Day 8	SACRIFICE: *I will die to my love of self.*	27
Day 9	HUMILITY: *I will lay down my pride for you.*	29
Day 10	VULNERABILITY: *I will confess my sins.*	31
Day 11	REPENTANCE: *I will seek your forgiveness.*	33
Day 12	PRIORITY: *I will forsake all others for you.*	35
Day 13	ROMANCE: *I will continue to date you.*	37
Day 14	HONESTY: *I will never mislead you.*	39
Day 15	AFFIRMATION: *I will encourage you daily.*	41
Day 16	ESTEEM: *I will value you and your opinion.*	43
Day 17	COMMUNICATION: *I will not shut you out.*	45
Day 18	WISE COUNSEL: *I will trust your advice.*	47
Day 19	ACCOUNTABILITY: *I will heed your warnings.*	49
Day 20	UNDERSTANDING: *I will respect your feelings.*	51
Day 21	PRAYER: *I will pray with you and over you.*	53
Day 22	WORSHIP: *I will glorify the Lord with you.*	55
Day 23	MINISTRY: *I will serve others alongside you.*	57
Day 24	GIFTS: *I will encourage your spiritual gifts.*	59
Day 25	HOLINESS: *I will celebrate the changes you make.*	61

Day 26	EMPATHY: *I will identify with your struggles.*	63
Day 27	COMPASSION: *I will help you cope with trials.*	65
Day 28	HUMOR: *I will cheer you up with laughter.*	67
Day 29	CONNECTION: *I will make quality time for you.*	69
Day 30	PEACE: *I will resolve conflict quickly with you.*	71
Day 31	IN-LAWS: *I will love your family as my own.*	73
Day 32	RESPECT: *I will teach our children to honor you.*	75
Day 33	UNITY: *I will ensure we are on the same page.*	77
Day 34	TRUST: *I will give you the benefit of the doubt.*	79
Day 35	PRIVACY: *I will ensure you hear things first.*	81
Day 36	LIABILITY: *I will own the consequences of my actions.*	83
Day 37	ATTRACTION: *I will unconditionally desire you.*	85
Day 38	REVIVAL: *I will invest in strengthening our marriage.*	87
Day 39	INTIMACY: *I will respect your sexual boundaries.*	89
Day 40	PLEASURE: *I will put your desires before my own.*	91
Day 41	COMPANIONSHIP: *I will celebrate life's joys with you.*	93
Day 42	COMFORT: *I will console you in your suffering.*	95
Day 43	PATIENCE: *I will be patient with you.*	97
Day 44	GRACE: *I will bless you when you least deserve it.*	99
Day 45	FORGIVENESS: *I will not hold your sins against you.*	101
Day 46	IDENTITY: *I will affirm who you are in Christ.*	103
Day 47	DEFENSE: *I will guard you from persecution.*	105
Day 48	TEAMWORK: *I will share the workload in our home.*	107
Day 49	FRIENDSHIP: *I will make you my closest confidante.*	109
Day 50	KINDNESS: *I will not use my words to harm you.*	111
Day 51	SYMPATHY: *I will care for you when you are sick.*	113
Day 52	LOYALTY: *I will love you till death do us part.*	115
	Postface	117
	Resources	119
	About The Author	123

PREFACE

Eternally Grateful

My wife, Amber, is amazing! She is beautiful inside and out, true to her faith in Christ, a fantastic wife and mother, and easily the most compassionate woman I have ever known. She is the epitome of sweet, southern charm but 100% authentic. Words cannot describe all she means to me because of what we have been through together. For over 23-years, we have defended our marriage against divorce and navigated difficult trials to keep our family strong. To say our marital journey has been easy would be a lie. God has carried us through the fire many times, but He has also given us renewed appreciation for the gift of a second chance to redeem and restore our broken marriage.

Amber and I dated for 5-months before getting engaged. We waited an additional 3-months before walking down the aisle. I often joke that I had to get her under contract fast before some other guy did. We met after graduating college and quickly knew we wanted to spend the rest of our lives together. Loving her was effortless but knowing how to be a great husband proved to be a challenge. As a naïve 23-year-old, I was anxious to begin my life with her. However, I was so consumed with getting to the wedding chapel that I failed to seriously consider what I was committing to when I officially said, "I do."

When I think back to our wedding, I can remember so many details: Amber's wedding dress, gorgeous smile, and big, green eyes for one. I remember singing to her during the ceremony, though she did not shed a tear so as not to ruin her make-up. I can recall songs the musicians played, how packed that country church was, and the preacher's voice as he spoke. I treasure those memories because they remind me of how happy we were on that day. Nevertheless (and regretfully so), I cannot entirely remember the vows I recited. Certainly, I meant what I said, but the details are fuzzy because I treated them as a wedding formality rather than words I would live by till the day I died.

It pains me to admit that I said, "I do," yet walked away without a clue as to what I committed to accomplishing. All I had were naïve promises to do my best and love her forever. The problem was my ignorance of what God expected from me. I knew how to love myself. I was an expert in that area, but knowing what sacrificial love looked like from God's perspective was an afterthought. Fast forward 23-years later and it is all I think about because I have the scars to prove it. I thought I knew what it meant to truly love my wife as Christ loves the church, but I was too prideful to ask for help.

What God taught me is that to be a godly husband and father, **"He must increase, but I must decrease" (John 3:30)**. In other words, I cannot be the man He calls me to be unless I die to my love of self, take up my cross, and follow Jesus. That means I must not only pray to Him daily but obey His teachings so I can fulfill His will for my life. Scripture is full of wisdom on how to love my wife, but it is meaningless if I do not apply what it teaches to my heart. That is why I created this devotional—to provide a starting point for couples to discover how to love their spouse daily and fulfill their wedding vows.

That is not to say Amber and I have it all figured out. We struggle applying God's standard of righteousness every day. We are thankful, though, for His grace and mercy because He saved our marriage. We are not perfect, but our mindset is focused on being a godly husband and wife to each other. Tomorrow is not guaranteed, so we try to make the most of our time together and allow the Lord to refine our personal character. Outside of salvation, being married to Amber is God's greatest blessing to me. She is my precious angel, and I cannot imagine life without her. That is why knowing how to love her is crucial, so I can be the husband God calls me to be by loving her sacrificially.

INTRODUCTION

True Love Defined

For many of us, our wedding day is a distant blur. We can recall how nervous we felt leading up to the ceremony or how relieved we were when the anxiety was behind us, but it is difficult to remember every detail as time passes. Wedding vows tend to fall into the category of flashbacks we remember, generally-speaking, as it can be difficult to articulate how we felt many years later. What we often recall are the vows we were asked to repeat: "In good times and in bad, in sickness and in health, as long as we both shall live." Thus, the greater question is not whether we remember our vows as time passes but if we fully understood what we pledged to our spouse in the first place.

When we think about marriage vows, we often view them through a lens of "I do" rather than "I will!" Keep in mind, "I do" is a statement of agreement to the officiator's question: "Do You?" There is no call to action in that moment but an acknowledgement of commitment to each other till death do us part. The challenge is we often shift into trial by fire mode once the honeymoon ends and expect our spouse to know what we are thinking and feeling. Unfortunately, the door swings both ways as we blend our individual lives into one cohesive unit. It is no easy task. Therefore, we must show patience and understanding toward one another to avoid conflict and dissension.

Thankfully, the Lord has given us incredible wisdom to navigate the stormy seas of marriage. We do not want to merely survive life's trials but thrive in fulfilling our covenant. As with any endeavor, spiritual growth begins with surrender to God's authority, submission to His sovereign will, and obedience to His Word. They are the foundational pillars of success for every aspect of our faith journey. In turn, we must humble ourselves and ask the Lord to teach us how to be better husbands and wives, respectively. Otherwise, we will work from our own personal strength rather than allow the Spirit to direct our steps.

If we study the book of Hosea, we will find God making numerous "I will" statements to His people despite their repetitive sin. That blueprint is incredibly valuable because it paints a backdrop for how we should honor and cherish our spouse. For if we do not know how to love sacrificially, how will we avoid becoming frustrated? Even our best intentions will never help us achieve peace and harmony if we do not know what the Lord expects from us on our wedding day. That is why we must shift our perspective from "I do" to "I will!" to better understand the defining characteristics of a God-honoring marriage.

Many failed marriages could have been avoided had they known how to love their spouse like Christ loves the church. Granted, none of us will ever reach perfection. We all need salvation, but that does not excuse our lack of knowledge or inability to make a head-to-heart connection by applying what Scripture teaches. Rather, we must define the attributes of a godly marriage and put a plan of action in place to serve our spouse sacrificially. For Jesus is our ultimate example, and we are wise to emulate how He loved His bride, the church. Failure to do so will only allow discontentment to flourish and bait us to question whether we were meant to be married in the first place.

No marriage should end in divorce if we commit to do whatever it takes to love our spouse sacrificially. Granted, we will make mistakes along the way and suffer the consequences of our foolishness, but that does not mean we can plead ignorance for not knowing how to love our spouse. God gave us His Word to guide our behavior, and we must apply what it teaches every day of our lives. Marriage is one of God's greatest blessings to humanity. Thus, let us appreciate His precious gift by not merely agreeing to love our spouse till death do us part but putting our heart's devotion into action to the glory of Jesus' name.

PROLOGUE

Finding a Rhythm

The beauty of this devotional is that it is flexible. You can utilize it based on your respective schedule. The key is finding a consistent rhythm that works for your marriage. Keep in mind, this book is not like most devotionals. I have included examples from my own life to help illustrate each topic and set the tone for vulnerability. Most self-help books tend to preach at you, but that is not what you will find throughout these pages. Instead, you will experience real and honest confessions designed to help you develop spiritual intimacy with your beloved spouse.

One thing I have learned shepherding discipleship groups is that few people will go far beneath the surface of their heart until they know it is safe to do so. That kind of confession and self-reflection is risky, which is why we tend to play it safe and resist opening up completely. It is also why I put my heart on the chopping block and shared details from my past across all 52-days of this resource. My prayer is that you will feel empowered to do likewise and communicate openly with your spouse. Vulnerability is never easy, but it is the secret ingredient to building a new foundation of oneness in your marriage.

The structure of this book provides four plans to choose from as you embark upon your journey together. Which option you choose is not critical because the key to success is consistency. So, before you begin, discuss what you feel is reasonable. Think about your respective schedules and decide what makes sense based on the commitments you keep. Most couples will fall in the 26-week to 52-week range, while others may look for something more intensive over a span of 13-weeks or even 52-days. In the end, it all comes down to what you will hold yourselves accountable to and how desperately you need help. What is most important is discerning which track works best for your marriage and then sticking to that plan until completion.

Relaxed: 52-weeks

Couples who choose the 52-week option are looking for a long-term solution to promote spiritual intimacy. If you have a weekly date night or can implement one, use this book as an opportunity to bring more connection and spiritual intimacy to your conversations.

Moderate: 26-weeks

Couples who choose the 26-week option will likely discuss 2-days of homework at once. It is the happy medium between short and long-term Bible study but requires discipline to build robust discussion into your routine. It is a great option to build consistency if you need help.

Intense: 13-weeks

Couples who choose the 13-week option will likely do this study in a small group format, but it is not for the faint of heart. It will require 4-days of homework with your spouse before meeting weekly to discuss in community. For couples who can plan their weekends wisely, 13-weeks is very attainable. 2-topics over 2-days. Discipline required.

Extreme: 52-days

Couples who choose the 52-day option are likely in desperate need of immediate help to fix their marriage or, on the opposite extreme, are mature enough in faith to handle a daily workload. Many couples will have dreams of knocking this study out in 52-days. However, it may not be feasible based on your schedules. Proceed with caution and do not bite off more than you can chew. Quality over quantity!

Seasons of Life

I would be remiss not to mention that those who read this book will find themselves at different crossroads based on their relationship status. As such, please allow me to encourage your heart as you begin to navigate through this devotional resource.

Single or Dating

If you are single or dating, this book is preparatory. You might find it difficult relating to each topic now, but please do not be discouraged. Lord-willing, one day you will reap the blessings of marriage and all the wisdom you treasured in your heart will produce a great harvest.

Engaged

If you are engaged, this book is akin to pre marital counseling. It will guide you on what to prioritize as you prepare for the future. Use it to promote dialogue on issues many couples take for granted. By learning how to talk openly together, you will know what God expects before you take your final step toward matrimony.

Newlywed

If you are newly married, you are likely working hard to find a rhythm and experiencing the trials and errors of living with an imperfect mate. The first years of marriage can be a fight for many couples. Therefore, before you get too far down the road, adjust and recalibrate your focus by using this book to help identify blind spots and areas of concern.

Married Without Kids

If you are married without kids, you have the unique opportunity to invest time, energy, and resources building a godly foundation for the future. Whether you choose to build a family or not, take full advantage of this "quieter" season of life to promote spiritual intimacy together.

Married With Kids

If you have started a family, you know how busy life can get and what a struggle it is to maintain a healthy marriage. Be encouraged and use this devotional to reveal which dead branches need pruning so that new growth can begin developing in your heart and marriage.

Empty Nested

If you are empty nested, getting to know your mate all over again can be frightening. Many couples divorce after their kids leave home because issues once brushed under the rug come to light. However, just because time has gone by doesn't mean that you cannot learn how to fall in love with your mate a second time. Enjoy the dating phase!

Divorced

If you are divorced, this devotional will be a difficult read. It will shed light on factors which ultimately led to your marital demise, but it can also help you reconcile the past and move forward. Embrace the fresh perspective this book offers as you consider the plans God has for your future, especially if you choose to marry again.

Widowed

If you widowed, life has not turned out how you once imagined, but you can celebrate your marital covenant for the time God allowed you to share together. Whether or not you marry again, consider using this book as an opportunity to reflect upon all you learned through the years as you discern what the Lord has in store moving forward.

Day 1 – Devotion

I will love you with all my heart.

> *"I have loved you with an everlasting love;
> therefore I have continued my faithfulness to you."*
>
> — Jeremiah 31:3 —

How often do we love our spouse unconditionally? Do we expect a reward for our effort or is our love selflessly motivated? Satan thrives when expectations abound because he makes us think we need to give something to get something in return. It can be a recipe for disaster in a marriage because Biblical love is not manipulative but sacrificial. Our intentions will either glorify God or ourselves, so our motives must be pure and holy to avoid seeking selfish gain. There is no greater blessing than to love, honor, and cherish our spouse until death do us part. Yet, as time goes by, love can easily be assumed. Thus, we must ensure our heart's devotion is not lost in translation but plain as day so there is no room to doubt our true intentions.

I would like to say my love for Amber has been unconditional over the course of our marriage, but for many years I was too prideful and stubborn to recognize my selfishness. I was blind to my own blindness yet acted as if I could clearly see. I thought I was a good husband who loved his wife selflessly, but I was just manipulating her heart without realizing it. For example, if I cooked dinner, cleaned the house, and put the kids to bed, she felt loved. However, if I expected sex in return, I was actually self-funneling and not loving her sacrificially like Jesus would. I wanted to believe I was serving her needs and putting her first in my heart. More often than not, it was all for my benefit because I expected my desires to be met as a reward for my efforts. I manipulated love for selfish gain, and I deeply regret putting my fleshly desires before her.

Heart motivation plays a key role in the health of a marriage. If we think we can play our cards right to get what we want, we will miss out on the true joy of marriage which compels us to love sacrificially. God never intended for marriage to be self-serving. Rather, He gave us the capacity to love because it is a defining attribute of His holy character. Christ died on the cross for our sins because He loved us, not because we deserved it. He did not sacrifice Himself because He expected anything in return either. Rather, He chose to love us because His focus was on our needs, not His own. Therefore, we are wise to learn from His example so that we do not miss the forest through the trees and position our desires above loving our spouse with pure devotion.

Application

1. What do you love most about your spouse? Why?
2. Why are expectations so dangerous to the health of a marriage?
3. How often do you love your spouse through a self-funneling filter? What needs to change to love them sacrificially instead?
4. How has God redeemed your heart and taught you that it is better to give love to your spouse than receive it?
5. What does loving your spouse with all your heart look like to you? How is your perspective different from your spouse's?

Reflection

"Love is patient and kind; love does not envy or boast; it is not arrogant or rude. It does not insist on its own way; it is not irritable or resentful; it does not rejoice at wrongdoing but rejoices with the truth. Love bears all things, believes all things, hopes all things, endures all things."

— *1 Corinthians 13:4–7* —

Day 2 – Commitment

I will never leave or forsake you.

*"To the married I give this charge (not I, but the Lord):
the wife should not separate from her husband (but if she does,
she should remain unmarried or else be reconciled to her husband),
and the husband should not divorce his wife."*

— 1 Corinthians 7:10–11 —

Divorce is a big issue in marriage today. For many couples, having an escape clause is justifiable if our desires are not being met or we are unhappy. We marry assuming the other person will fill a void which is missing within us. The problem is that life can get messy when the person we fell in love with becomes a shell of their former self. Time reveals the good, bad, and ugly of who we are and leaves our mate with a critical choice. Should I stay or should I go? The Bible does offer two justifiable reasons for divorce (adultery and abandonment by an unbeliever), but they are reserved in the event there is a complete lack of repentance and heart change for such behavior.

Scripture is clear that the Lord hates divorce. Marriage reflects Jesus' devotion to His bride, the church, and He promised to never abandon or forsake us. There is no sin big enough to separate us from His love, and He expects that we emulate the same level of commitment in our marital covenant as well. Are there days when we are tired and weary of our spouse? Sure. Does the enemy tempt us with the promise of greener pastures if we just give up? Always! However, the reason Satan wants us to abandon our mate is because he knows how vulnerable we are when isolated. In turn, we must remain committed to one another.

Our marriage almost ended in divorce. Sin had taken such a strong hold over me that I threw it all away to see if the grass was greener on the other side. It did not take too long for me to realize what a horrendous decision I had made, and I went into hiding because of it. Guilt, shame, and regret were so intense that I isolated myself from my wife out of fear. I did not want to face the consequences of my actions, but God opened my eyes and I chose to confess my adultery.

Our marriage came to a screeching halt the day I confessed, but Amber did not walk away. Instead, she agreed to walk through Biblical counseling together, and God redeemed our marriage. Despite the immeasurable weight of spiritual warfare, she refused to let the enemy win. Amber faced the biggest decision of her life and had every reason to divorce me, but she didn't. Instead, she chose to take what the enemy meant for evil and turn it for good, and her decision to never forsake me is a testimony of God's amazing grace in creating beauty from ashes.

Application

1. Define what commitment looks like to you. Why does it matter?
2. How has divorce impacted your life (directly or indirectly)? What has God taught you about commitment because of it?
3. Why is your spouse's marital commitment to you such a blessing?
4. What changes can you make to divorce-proof your marriage?
5. How often do you wonder if the grass is greener on the other side? Why is it so dangerous to give thought to the idea?

Reflection

"If a man vows a vow to the LORD or swears an oath to bind himself by a pledge, he shall not break his word. He shall do according to all that proceeds out of his mouth."

— Numbers 30:2 —

Day 3 – Security

I will guard and protect you.

*"Fear not, for I am with you; be not dismayed, for I am your God;
I will strengthen you, I will help you, I will uphold you
with my righteous right hand."*

— Isaiah 41:10 —

There is no greater gift than knowing we are safe from harm in the arms of Jesus. Similarly, there is no greater privilege in marriage than providing our spouse complete assurance that we will protect them. Safety comes in many forms. We tend to think of protection as physical but spiritually is where most couples struggle. We assume that we are strong enough to resist temptation, so we lower our guard rather than solidify our defense via prayer and Bible study. Truly, nothing will cause our spouse more mental and emotional anguish than us yielding to temptation, for sin calls into question whether we can be trusted. It also opens the door for spiritual warfare to flourish when we escape to idolatry and entertainment for security instead of God.

I secretly brought an addiction to pornography into our marriage. Because I had not dealt with it before our wedding day, nor confessed it, Amber had no idea I was enslaved to lust and allowed immorality to flourish in my mind. All she had was my vow to protect her which eventually proved to be false. I allowed the enemy to take residence in our home because of my sin, and he attacked our marriage relentlessly until I threw all caution to the wind and had an affair. The amount of spiritual warfare I unleashed upon her was immeasurable. I hurt her in ways I will never fully comprehend. However, God protected her in ways I never could because His love never fails. She found security in the arms of Jesus, and His love enabled her to give our marriage a second chance so I could change and become a godly husband.

Allowing the Lord to overhaul our personal character is not an easy task, but it is the only way to guard our hearts from temptation. Our spouse deserves to know that we will not enter into temptations as eager and willing participants. Rather, they need reassurance that we will be watchful and sober-minded (1 Peter 5:8) to protect them. We often forget that sin has a ripple effect on others. What we allow to infiltrate our minds directly impacts our behavior. Therefore, if we fail to protect ourselves, what makes us think we can guard those whom God has entrusted to our care? Our spouse's heart is a precious gift, so we must do everything in our power to protect them from harm by handling our own business and not giving the enemy a foothold.

Application

1. What does it mean to spiritually protect your spouse? What are the dangers of not taking that threat seriously?
2. How have you failed your spouse by not guarding your own heart?
3. How have you allowed Satan to enter your home uninvited? Where do you need to clean house to protect your family?
4. Why is it important to wash your mind with the truth of Scripture? How can God's Word keep you from yielding to temptation?
5. How have you seen the Lord miraculously guard your marriage?

Reflection

"We who are strong have an obligation to bear with the failings of the weak, and not to please ourselves. Let each of us please his neighbor for his good, to build him up."

— Romans 15:1–2 —

Day 4 – Provision

I will provide for our family's needs.

> *"But if anyone does not provide for his relatives,*
> *and especially for members of his household,*
> *he has denied the faith and is worse than an unbeliever."*
>
> — 1 Timothy 5:8 —

Survival is all about maintaining four essentials: fire, shelter, water, and food. No matter where we live, we cannot survive without these basic necessities. When we think of provision, though, money becomes our focus. How will we generate income? Who will work to earn it? Will we have enough to pay our bills? There are many questions surrounding finances that can cause stress and dissension in the home, and Satan knows it. That is why he tempts us to live beyond our means and pursue money, power, status, and fame to achieve true happiness. The more we buy into provision being physical vs. spiritual, the easier it will be to lose sight of what is critically important to preserve a God-honoring home: love, time, and attention.

We cannot ignore our duty to care for the needs of our family. We must work to earn income but also care for the spiritual formation of our children, because God deems those duties mandatory. However, what is more important is how we invest our time loving one another in spirit and truth. A godly home begins with surrendering to Biblical authority and aligning our will with God's sovereignty, but how we apply His Word is paramount. In other words, we cannot say that we love our family but not invest time, energy, and resources proving it. We must provide far more than a paycheck. Rather, we must love them with grace and mercy because God expects us to pay forward what He has given to us through salvation in Christ.

One of the keys to our marriage's success has been finding common ground as it relates to money and finances. We have learned to live on one income vs. two which protects us from living beyond our means in the event something tragic happens. Amber homeschools our girls, but I have resisted chasing the corporate ladder so my time is maximized at home. As long as my income takes care of our needs, I believe my time is better served at home where Amber and I can be more involved ministering to our girls and shepherding their hearts unto the Lord. One of the greatest decisions I ever made was being content with God's financial provision rather than thinking we needed more to be happy. It has allowed me to comfortably say, "No," to promotional opportunities which could have monopolized my time and inevitably hurt my family. God has blessed us beyond measure, but we believe it is due to making Him our top priority instead of chasing after the pleasures of this world for selfish gain.

Application

1. Do you believe you are a good provider? Why or why not?
2. In what ways do you and your spouse each provide for your family?
3. How has money become a wedge of dissension in your marriage?
4. How has God blessed your discipline around finances by working together? If not, what changes do you need to make?

Reflection

"God is not mocked, for whatever one sows, that will he also reap. For the one who sows to his own flesh will from the flesh reap corruption, but the one who sows to the Spirit will from the Spirit reap eternal life."

— Galatians 6:7–8 —

Day 5 – Burdens

I will carry you when you are weary.

"Bear one another's burdens and so fulfill the law of Christ."
— *Galatians 6:2* —

In every marriage, there comes a point where we vow to love our spouse in good times and in bad, in sickness and in health. Whether it be a common cold or a terminal health diagnosis, God expects us to step into the gap and take on the burden of responsibility to care for our beloved. We compensate for them when they are tired and carry them when they are weary. It is an honor and privilege to be the hands and feet of Jesus when our spouse is physically, mentally, emotionally, and spiritually spent. For when fear, doubt, and worry overwhelm their psyche, we fight the enemy in their place. We must also stand guard at the doorway of despair and remind them that they are safe and secure in Jesus when hopelessness seeks to devour their mind.

It can be difficult watching our beloved suffer. Sometimes, our best is just not good enough to calm their nerves and bring peace to their troubled soul. Only Christ can save, so it is our job to bathe them in prayer and the healing waters of Scripture. Oftentimes, we want to be our spouse's savior when all they really need is love and support until death do us part. The more we sacrifice our time, energy, and resources to serve them in their hour of need, the more we glorify the One who will heal them from calamity when they enter His presence one day. Truly, there is no greater joy than loving our spouse when they are low and lifting their eyes to heaven by pointing them to Jesus.

Losing a child is one of the worst feelings a couple can experience. After the birth of our oldest two daughters, pregnancies took a toll on Amber's physical health. Her progesterone levels plummeted to zero and getting pregnant again became impossible. God closed her womb for 8-years until He enabled her to get pregnant again. She gave birth to our third daughter so we tried for another, but God had other plans. Her pregnancy ended in miscarriage after 11-weeks and she was forced to reconcile that perhaps the end had come to have more children.

In the aftermath of a miscarriage, many emotions come pouring out. Why did this happen? Could it have been prevented? Our hearts were broken, but God brought us closer together by giving perspective through it all. What we learned is that He is always in control. In His sovereignty we lost a child, but in His grace He blessed us with yet another pregnancy and our fourth daughter. We never expected to have more than two children after our season of barrenness, but God saw fit that we finish with four girls who have blessed us beyond measure. We lost a child along the way, but His plans were far greater than we ever expected.

Application

1. Give an example of a burden your spouse is or was carrying. How did you minister to them despite their pain and suffering?
2. Why is it critical to point your spouse to Jesus when they are overwhelmed with fear, doubt, and worry? Why not solve it yourself?
3. What are residual benefits of carrying your spouse's burdens?
4. Which of your spouse's burdens can you begin carrying that you are not already? How so?

Reflection

"Two are better than one, because they have a good reward for their toil. For if they fall, one will lift up his fellow. But woe to him who is alone when he falls and has not another to lift him up!"

— *Ecclesiastes 4:9–10* —

Day 6 – Gentleness

I will shepherd your heart.

> *"Likewise, husbands, live with your wives in an understanding way, showing honor to the woman as the weaker vessel, since they are heirs with you of the grace of life, so that your prayers may not be hindered."*
>
> — 1 Peter 3:7 —

Gentleness is not a character attribute many of us possess today. Rather, it is a fruit of the Spirit given by God to those who obey His Word and apply it to their lives. From a marital perspective, wives are to be treated with the utmost care and concern by their husbands, which means gentleness is a precious commodity. A man cannot live with his wife in an understanding way if he does not honor and cherish her like fine China or crystal. Keep in mind, she is not weaker from a value perspective. Quite the opposite! She is an equal heir to the grace of life. Therefore, a husband must speak to his wife's heart and mind with gentleness, because God created women differently to complement their husbands in the marital relationship.

Likewise, wives are to use gentle discretion as they submit to their husband's authority. Just as the church submits to the authority of Christ, wives are to emulate the same respect regarding their husband's leadership. Submission can be a wedge of dissension in the home when it is made begrudgingly. However, if we consider how a husband is called to submit to the authority of Jesus, it is easier to understand that gentleness and submission are not exclusive of one another but complementary. We are on far more equal ground than we realize in marriage because God expects us to love and respect each other as fellow heirs of His immeasurable grace. For the husband is called to model submission unto Christ, and likewise, the wife to her husband as God's Word teaches.

Shepherding my wife's heart means being sensitive to her feelings when God calls her to submit to my headship. I am certainly imperfect and have made many decisions without seeking her opinion. There are definitive reasons why submitting to a sinful husband like me has been difficult for Amber. I completely broke her trust! How then could she submit to my authority after all I put her through? It has not been easy, but her submission is not to me. Rather, she submits to Jesus through me. My job is to model submission unto Christ so she knows my life is led by prayer, humility, and obedience to the truth of God's Word. I must also love her with patience and understanding because submission is difficult. It is a sacrificial gift of love, not an expectation. As such, I must shepherd her heart with gentleness and respect because her submission is a precious gift that I do not deserve but am eternally grateful for, all things considered.

Application

1. Would you consider yourself a gentle spouse? Why or why not?
2. Are you more gentle toward your spouse or children? How so?
3. In what ways would being more gentle toward your spouse benefit your marriage?
4. How has submission been difficult to apply in your home?
5. What scars do you bear from seasons of trial where gentleness was lacking? What did you learn from those experiences?

Reflection

"Likewise, wives, be subject to your own husbands, so that even if some do not obey the word, they may be won without a word by the conduct of their wives, when they see your respectful and pure conduct."

— 1 Peter 3:1–2 —

Day 7 – Self-Control

I will pursue godliness daily.

> *"For this very reason, make every effort to supplement your faith with virtue, and virtue with knowledge, and knowledge with self-control, and self-control with steadfastness, and steadfastness with godliness, and godliness with brotherly affection, and brotherly affection with love."*
>
> — 2 Peter 1:5–7 —

Self-control is arguably our greatest asset to achieving godliness. It enables us to quit yielding to temptation and ensures we are living for righteousness in every facet of our lives. Self-control helps keep our emotions in check and stops us from saying things we would otherwise regret as well. It is the great equalizer to anger as we diffuse conflict in the home. It is also our spiritual accountability to conform us into the image of Christ. Self-control can actually save our marriage from ruin if we filter our thoughts and emotions through Scripture. It helps us pause and think before we act so we avoid saying or doing something we might ultimately regret. Godly marriages are won or lost on the battlefield of temptation, but self-control proves whether we will yield to fleshly desires or remain obedient to Christ.

Amber and I have experienced the gauntlet of emotional outbursts as parents. We are blessed with daughters who are respectful and obey instruction. However, they are imperfect and test our patience like all children do. We have done well managing our emotions, most often, but have also struggled venting our anger and frustration at times. The challenge is that we feed off each other. If my emotions are running high, hers are impacted and vice versa. Rather than balance each other out, we often pile on top of one another. Before we know it, we are in conflict not because of what the kids have done to push our buttons but for losing self-control altogether. It is a vicious cycle. Nevertheless, being accountable to each *other for our actions has allowed us to gain self-control rather than lose it entirely.*

The real question we must wrestle with is whether we know how to control ourselves. We often let feelings dictate our behavior instead of the Spirit of God who dwells within us. Why? At what point did we become so wise in our own eyes that we no longer required the Lord's wisdom nor our spouse's intervention? Satan has convinced us that we are better off hedging our own bet than asking for help, but our poor track record proves how ill-equipped we are to remain holy and avoid foolishness. As such, we must remain steadfast in our faith commitment because the Lord empowers us to pursue godliness. Our homes will never be peaceful without self-control, for it holds us accountable and guards our hearts from yielding to temptation. It will not be joyful, either, if we do not filter our emotions through the Bible for wisdom, clarity, and discernment.

Application

1. How has a lack of self-control negatively impacted your marriage and caused you to regret your foolish behavior?
2. In what ways has self-control saved you from letting your emotions get the best of you during conflict resolution?
3. Why is self-control an easy target for Satan to attack in your life?
4. How has God blessed your marriage by being self-controlled?

Reflection

"But the fruit of the Spirit is love, joy, peace, patience, kindness, goodness, faithfulness, gentleness, self-control; against such things there is no law."

— Galatians 5:22–23 —

Day 8 – Sacrifice

I will die to my love of self.

> *"Do nothing from selfish ambition or conceit, but in humility count others more significant than yourselves. Let each of you look not only to his own interests, but also to the interests of others."*
>
> — Philippians 2:3–4 —

When we strip away the façade of self-righteousness, what we are left with is a sad realization that we love ourselves far more than God, our spouse, or anyone else. Love of self is the root of all evil in our lives. It assumes our wants and desires are the only things which matter and baits us into believing we are the center of the universe. No husband or wife will ever achieve happiness in their marriage if love of self takes precedence. There are simply too many variables conflicting in the home to not yield to one another as the Spirit leads. Granted, we all have needs and desires, but they cannot be one in the same for a marriage to survive. Rather, we must meet one another's needs and, if appropriate, attempt to satisfy personal desires as well.

I never knew about love of self before entering Biblical counseling. One session, our counselor asked if I had read a particular resource. I said, "Yes." He asked about another and my response was the same. At that moment, he stopped and said plainly, "Well, I can safely say you have a disconnect between your head and heart. Your problem is love of self. You love yourself more than God, your wife, your kids, or anyone else." His blunt words cut like a knife. I had never thought of it that way, but he was right. Love of self was the root of my struggles, not sexual immorality. For years, I tried solving my sin addiction through behavior modification, but what I really needed was open heart surgery to extract the cancer of wickedness within me. God took a sledgehammer to my pride, but I finally realized why I had never found victory before.

The true danger of selfishness exists below the surface of our hearts in the dark shadows of motivation. As mentioned previously, too many couples fail to see how selfish motives undermine good intentions. It leaves our spouse feeling manipulated instead of loved. Assumptions and expectations wreak havoc on good intentions. If we assume our intentions are pure and expect a return for our good deeds, we are not serving sacrificially out of love but living for ourselves. Satan is a master manipulator and he will keep us focused on the fruit of our sins rather than the root of our problems. As a result, we must guard against putting personal interests above our spouse, for conditional love is nothing more than a manipulation tool designed to satisfy guilty pleasures. The more we die to our love of self, the greater chance we will love our spouse like Jesus would and resist temptation.

Application

1. Do you see love of self as your biggest problem? Why or why not?
2. What is causing a disconnect between your head and heart?
3. How are you succeeding at loving your spouse selflessly?
4. How have expectations hindered your efforts to love your spouse?
5. What sacrifices could you begin making to put your spouse's needs above your guilty pleasures?

Reflection

"In the same way, husbands should love their wives as their own bodies. He who loves his wife loves himself. For no one ever hated his own flesh, but nourishes and cherishes it, just as Christ does the church."

— *Ephesians 5:28–29* —

Day 9 – Humility

I will lay down my pride for you.

*"For everyone who exalts himself will be humbled,
and he who humbles himself will be exalted."*

— Luke 14:11 —

Humility is about seeking opportunities to humble ourselves daily. It is not a gift we receive or something we can purchase. Instead, it is an intentional act of lowering our posture and position by elevating someone's needs above our own. In the crucible of marriage, humility is about living sacrificially to love, honor, and cherish our spouse. It is not self-serving but focused on blessing our spouse so they know their interests and opinions take higher precedence than ours. It removes us from a self-serving pedestal and positions us at the back of the line vs. upfront. Granted, humility is easier said than done, but it is necessary to create an environment which promotes true vulnerability.

Too many marriages suffer because pride fuels selfish desires. We cannot begin to display humility if we fail to recognize our loved one's needs as more important than our own. Satan always wants us to look out for our own interests, first and foremost. However, we must resist the urge to default into "me-first" mode and look for real opportunities to bless our spouse. Humility is never easy. It is one of the most difficult character attributes to master because it requires us to step outside our comfort zone and serve others like Jesus would. What we often miss is that pride must be broken for humility to take root, and the Lord will take matters into His own hands if we refuse to lay down our pride and humble ourselves. That is why Jesus' sacrifice is so powerful. He willingly went to the cross and humbled Himself for us, and we must do likewise if we expect to have a happy and healthy marriage.

I sometimes wonder what Amber saw in me when we got married. I was a confidant, young man with a hunger to prove himself and climb the corporate ladder. I was successful but prideful as well, and my naïve attitude caused me to think too highly of myself. I preferred things be done my way and let my opinion be known. To Amber's credit, she had an opinion too and did not shy away from speaking her mind when I held my ground. We argued over insignificant issues like paint colors and furniture, which made the early years of our marriage a grind. I was too stubborn to relent my opinion and it caused unnecessary tension in our home. Had I humbled myself and allowed her opinion to be heard, we could have avoided much conflict. I was too prideful, though, and it clearly showed when I had to be right all the time. What a fool I was, for I did not realize how I was hurting my wife by refusing to humble myself daily.

Application

1. Would you consider yourself a prideful person? Why or why not?
2. Give an example from your marriage of a time when you humbled yourself. What did you learn from that experience?
3. How has the enemy used pride to drive a wedge in your marriage?
4. In what ways could you humble yourself more to love, honor, and cherish your spouse?

Reflection

"If my people who are called by my name humble themselves and pray and seek my face and turn from their wicked ways, then I will hear from heaven and will forgive their sin and heal their land."

— 2 Chronicles 7:14 —

Day 10 – Vulnerability

I will confess my sins to you.

> "Therefore, confess your sins to one another and pray for one another, that you may be healed. The prayer of a righteous person has great power as it is working."
>
> — James 5:16 —

How often are we vulnerable with our spouse? Rarely, sometimes, or always? It is truly an important question to consider because confession is one of the most difficult spiritual disciplines to learn, and vulnerability is the path to get us there, not transparency. When we are transparent with our spouse, we reveal truths about our past to the extent in which we feel comfortable. Mentally, we draw a line in the sand and vow to never cross it, no matter how much damage it may cause. However, vulnerability challenges us to share our thoughts and feelings without knowing how they will be received. It is risky but also freeing, because it forces us out of darkness and into the light of grace and mercy where true healing is found.

Confession was never meant to be easy. It requires self-recognition and ownership of sins which is humbling. It is the doorway to freedom, though, because it forces us out of isolation where Satan holds us captive. Why then do we avoid it? Unfortunately, we often refrain from sharing insecurities and failures with our spouse. For whatever reason, we act as if we are doing them a favor by sparing them the details of how, where, and why we are struggling. A stronghold is solidified in our heart when we remain in hiding. Keep in mind, Satan wants us to avoid vulnerability in marriage because he knows that if we confess our sins, spiritual intimacy will increase and bring us closer together. That is why we must live in the light of truth and not hide in the dark shadows of deception and self-protection.

Sometimes, confession seems illogical. After I confessed my affair to Amber, I called a close friend who led a men's group I attended. He had not previously known about the adultery, so it came as a shock when I told him what I had done and that I confessed my sins to my wife. His response, though, was unexpected. He said, "I wish you had told me first (before telling Amber) so I could have talked you out of it." His reasoning? He did not know anyone who had confessed an affair and their marriage not end in divorce. In his mind, I should have reconciled with God and taken it to my grave because confession does not always work out. Needless to say, I did not agree with his perspective. Nevertheless, it taught me a lesson that confession is not about protecting myself but honoring God. The Lord called me to repent of my sins and make amends with my wife, and I am forever glad I did.

Application

1. In which areas of your life are you transparent (playing it safe) vs. being vulnerable (risking it all)? Why?
2. How has vulnerability brought your marriage closer together?
3. Why are you more prone to self-protect than confess your sins to your spouse? How can you change your fearful attitude?
4. Why would you take certain sins to the grave vs. confess them to those you have sinned against? How is it beneficial in any way?

Reflection

"Whoever conceals his transgressions will not prosper, but he who confesses and forsakes them will obtain mercy. Blessed is the one who fears the LORD always, but whoever hardens his heart will fall into calamity."

— Proverbs 28:13–14 —

Day 11 – Repentance

I will seek your forgiveness.

"The Lord is not slow to fulfill his promise as some count slowness, but is patient toward you, not wishing that any should perish, but that all should reach repentance."

— 2 Peter 3:9 —

When we embrace vulnerability and confess our sins to one another, the opportunity for reconciliation comes full circle. No longer are we held captive by fear but empowered by the Holy Spirit to obey God's Word. Forgiveness is not always guaranteed in marriage. When we admit our failures, a weight is transferred from our shoulders to our spouse's. We release the burden of secrecy and exchange it for freedom, whereas they are given the unenviable task of bearing the weight of knowing how we sinned against them. It is often why we live in bondage to guilt, shame, and regret. Rather than allow our spouse to help us conquer past demons, we choose to self-protect and dig a deeper hole for ourselves by remaining in hiding.

Forgiveness is the first step in burying the hatchet. It is an opportunity to choose whether we will live in freedom or remain in bondage to sin. Forgiveness is the secret to a great marriage because it magnifies whether we recognize our depth of depravity. It shifts our perspective away from saying "I'm sorry," and compels us to ask, "Will you please forgive me?" The more we forgive, the more we will experience freedom. It does not mean that the memory of sin fades away but that we will love our spouse when they are least deserving, because we are no different. Reconciliation is a two-way street whereby we forgive freely, not begrudgingly, for it makes no sense to harbor resentment and bitterness. Instead, we must forgive our spouse so the Lord will never withhold forgiveness from us in return (Matt. 6:14-15).

When I finally addressed the eight-hundred-pound gorilla of secret sin, I felt free. I stepped out of darkness and into the light of truth. What I did not expect was that the gorilla did not miraculously go away. It merely shifted from my shoulders to Amber's. Once I confessed, she had to bear the weight of mental and emotional torment knowing exactly what I had done. The temptation for her to enact revenge and give me a taste of my own medicine was intense. Instead, she chose to forgive rather than seek retribution. In her darkest hours, Jesus carried her through the fires of hell and gave her the strength to forgive me and save our marriage. In retrospect, she would admit that forgiveness is still a daily exercise for her. It can be hard not filtering present-day sins through past transgressions. Even so, she knows that she is a sinner too and in need of a Savior, which empowers her to forgive me for my past (and present) sins as well.

Application

1. Which past sins do you hold over your spouse? Which of yours do they still hold over your head? Why?
2. How are you harboring anger and bitterness toward your spouse?
3. How has God blessed your marriage when you have truly repented of your sins to one another?
4. Are you more prone to say, "I'm sorry" or "Please forgive me" to your spouse? Why does it matter?

Reflection

"For if you forgive others their trespasses, your heavenly Father will also forgive you, but if you do not forgive others their trespasses, neither will your Father forgive your trespasses."

— *Matthew 6:14–15* —

Day 12 – Priority

I will forsake all others for you.

> "Let marriage be held in honor among all, and let the marriage bed be undefiled, for God will judge the sexually immoral and adulterous."
>
> — Hebrews 13:4 —

Most of us remember vowing to love, honor, and cherish our spouse on our wedding day, but how often do we intentionally forsake all others to ensure our marriage is continually protected? Male and female interactions are commonplace in our culture. We talk to members of the opposite sex every day at work, recreation, etc. It is impossible to avoid, but are we purposefully protecting our heart from yielding to temptation or naively welcoming it in? Are we fully aware of who we are sharing personal details with, or do we see no harm in emotionally connecting to another man or woman? Marriage can easily become compromised if we lower our guard and allow others to meet needs reserved only for our spouse. Thus, it is critical we stop and evaluate whether we are forsaking all others or welcoming temptation into our home without the slightest care or concern.

Forsaking all others means a great deal to me, all things considered. For example, I now avoid sharing personal stories about myself with other women and being overly-friendly. I steer clear of 1-on-1 interactions in the workplace with women or anywhere outside our home as well. I strategically try to have Amber or other men present if female interactions cannot be avoided because it protects my heart and honors my wife. I never want to compromise Amber's trust, because I know what it feels like to lose her confidence and how long it took to earn it back. The last thing I want to do is give her cause for concern and inadvertently hurt her. As such, setting up solid boundaries and being well-guarded has helped me guard against compromising my marriage vows again.

Adultery comes in many forms—physical, mental, and emotional. Rarely do we set out to enter into an adulterous relationship, yet it often happens. Why? What makes us think the grass is greener on the other side and that our spouse is the reason we are unhappy? The challenge is that we often evaluate marriage from a glass-half-empty perspective, perpetuating discontentment, and then imagine if the grass is greener on the other side. What we eventually discover is that the grass is greener where we water it. Thus, if we desire intimacy with our spouse, we must reinforce boundaries and forsake all others from compromising our covenant to each other. God's sovereign provision in marriage is that our spouse is all we need to be happy and content. The sooner we realize that critical truth, the better off we will be.

Application

1. How big of a priority is your spouse's peace of mind to you?
2. Which personal relationships are putting a strain on your marriage?
3. How have you guarded your heart and mind from looking outside your marriage for satisfaction and fulfillment?
4. In what ways can you make your marriage bed pure and holy?
5. How do you see your marriage today: glass-half-empty or glass-half-full? What changes can you make to improve your outlook?

Reflection

"But seek first the kingdom of God and his righteousness, and all these things will be added to you. Therefore do not be anxious about tomorrow, for tomorrow will be anxious for itself."

— Matthew 6:33–34 —

Day 13 – Romance

I will continue to date you.

"Yet you do not know what tomorrow will bring. What is your life? For you are a mist that appears for a little time and then vanishes."

— James 4:14 —

There is nothing more important than spending quality time with our spouse. Words cannot describe the blessing of being 1-on-1 and uninterrupted. If we have children, carving out time for romance can prove difficult, for not everyone can find or afford a babysitter. How then do we prioritize dating to keep our romantic fire from being extinguished? In many ways, a date can be just the right medicine to cure trials, at least for one night. It takes us back to the beginning of our relationship and reminds us of how much fun we had getting to know each other. Regrettably, we get so busy with life that we forget to prioritize dating. It can be easy to look in the rearview mirror and wonder how time got away from us, but it cannot deter us from righting the ship and changing course to pursue romance moving forward.

Money is not required to date. All we need is creativity and selfless motivation. Dating requires that we step outside our comfort zone and plan something special with our spouse's personal preferences in mind. It communicates that we have paid close attention to the things they enjoy and how we want to create a unique experience that blesses their heart, mind, and soul. Romance is critical to the health of a marriage because it is not dependent upon anything other than self-sacrifice. When we plan a special date for our spouse, it lets them know that we desire to keep the embers of love burning brightly. And when we spontaneously do something out of the ordinary to honor and bless them, it reveals how much we love and appreciate our time together.

Date nights are a challenge for us. Like most couples, we get into a routine and forget to prioritize time away from the kids to reconnect as a couple. Excuses aside, I know dating makes Amber feel special, and the last thing I want her to believe is that I do not care about investing time, energy, and resources into our marriage. She sacrifices so much homeschooling our girls. The least I can do is plan a date to let her know I appreciate her. Granted, romance does not have to be fancy, just authentic and creative. Some of our best dates have been ones where we have spent time planning out all the details. It lets us know how much we want to create a lasting memory and keep the fire burning bright in our marriage. That being said, spontaneous dates are some of our favorites as well, because we are willing to drop everything at a moment's notice to spend quality time together.

Application

1. Why is dating so critical to the health of your marriage?
2. Which excuses distract you from dating your spouse more often?
3. What are some of your favorite dating memories prior to getting engaged? What made them so special?
4. How would your spouse define romance? What are the differences and similarities between your definition compared to theirs?
5. What kind of romantic date would your spouse enjoy most? Why?

Reflection

"As an apple tree among the trees of the forest, so is my beloved among the young men. With great delight I sat in his shadow, and his fruit was sweet to my taste. He brought me to the banqueting house, and his banner over me was love."

— *Song of Solomon 2:3–4* —

Day 14 – Honesty

I will never mislead you.

> *"Lying lips are an abomination to the LORD,*
> *but those who act faithfully are his delight."*
>
> — *Proverbs 12:22* —

Conventional wisdom says, "Honesty is the best policy!" but how often do we find ourselves bending the truth to cover our tracks? Lying is a slippery slope. In one respect, we know it is wrong, yet we justify it if the moment deems necessary. For example, if we were to plan a surprise or purchase a gift for our spouse, lying seems reasonable to keep it a secret. However, where do we draw a line and avoid being manipulative? Does God want us to be honest with our spouse 100% of the time, or are their instances where lying is justified? It is a hot topic, yet the greater question is why would we allow dishonesty to exist at all if God wants us to always speak truth in love?

Lying is an easy trap. One little white lie can lead to another and stop us from discerning right from wrong when the lines around our conscience are blurred. In life, grey is a favorite color when it comes to morality. Black and white are too rigid, so we often use shades of grey to minimize guilt and justify lying as a necessary means to an end. The problem is that a godly marriage is only as strong as the level of honesty it maintains. In turn, truth in love must be a hill we are willing to die on rather than surrender to the enemy. The truth hurts sometimes, but that is why we must be gentle and loving towards our spouse and show grace to them as the Spirit leads.

No man wants to answer the question from his wife, "Honey, do I look fat in this dress?" It is a recipe for disaster! We can laugh at the honesty of that question because we have all been there at some point. However, we have also experienced the carnage of either not answering it or being too honest with our opinion. Amber has certainly asked me some form of that question through the years, but I have learned that how I answer her is far more important than what I necessarily say. Therefore, I must be gentle to ensure I am always shepherding her heart with utmost care.

Knowing how to speak truth in love requires softening the edges of my words to speak blessing into her heart. Pointing out how a dress takes away from her beautiful features is more easily accepted than giving a blunt and honest answer. It allows me to not mislead her but instead, answer her question in a way which builds up her self-esteem. Do I always succeed? Absolutely not, but I am learning how to speak to my wife in an understanding way which honors my vow to be 100% truthful with her while not tearing her down in the process.

Application

1. Do you believe lying is justified in certain situations? How so?
2. How have little white lies spiraled out of control in your marriage?
3. Is there such a thing as being too honest? Why or why not?
4. How has being open and honest with each other strengthened your marital covenant?
5. Why is living with your spouse in an understanding way so critical to speaking truth in love?

Reflection

"Do not lie to one another, seeing that you have put off the old self with its practices and have put on the new self, which is being renewed in knowledge after the image of its creator."

— *Colossians 3:9–10* —

Day 15 – Affirmation

I will encourage you daily.

"So if there is any encouragement in Christ, any comfort from love, any participation in the Spirit, any affection and sympathy, complete my joy by being of the same mind, having the same love, being in full accord and of one mind."

— *Philippians 2:1–2* —

When the trials of life overwhelm our spouse's heart and mind, it is our job to provide comfort and support in their hour of need. There is nothing more powerful than a word of encouragement when our soul is tired and weary. The enemy preys upon those who isolate themselves when they feel broken and defeated by whispering lies of hopelessness deep within their hearts. God created marriage for many reasons, but companionship was arguably one of the greatest. He knew Adam needed someone to share his life with, and Eve was the perfect solution because they complimented one another.

Oftentimes, the world makes us think we are alone and that no one can relate to our trials and struggles. That is why we need the promises of Scripture to remind us of who we are in Christ. Thankfully, our spouse can be the conduit for communicating that message, because encouragement has the power to rewire our minds during spiritual blackouts. It reconnects us to our true power source, Jesus Christ, and reminds us that He is our source of strength. Thus, the more we pray His promises over our spouse, the greater chance we will have to defeat the enemy and protect them from future harm.

I believe that affirmation is one of the greatest blessings we can give our spouse. The key is putting it into practice daily. Not too many days have gone by where I have failed to give Amber a word of encouragement. I am keenly aware that

Satan attacks her mind daily, so I make it a priority to affirm her identity in Christ by guarding her from fear, doubt, and worry. I never want her to lose sight that she is God's beloved daughter. She is simply too precious to me not to point her directly to Jesus as her source of strength when she needs encouragement.

I know that my wife often tends to look at herself from a glass-half-empty perspective. She sees every imperfection and knows what she would like to change about herself if she could. As a result, I try to remind her of how blessed I am to be her husband and how perfect she is in my eyes. I provide no ammunition to support her negativity. Rather, I reaffirm her beauty so that she is never tempted to doubt my love. Granted, it does not always change how she sees herself, but it guards her heart and mind from spiritual warfare and redirects her attention to God's definition of strength and beauty as a woman (Prov. 31:10-31).

Application

1. Why is affirmation critical to maintaining a healthy marriage?
2. Which words of affirmation does your spouse need to hear daily from you to protect their heart and mind?
3. Why is it easier to remember critical words than words of blessing?
4. In what ways have you failed as your spouse's biggest encourager?
5. How can you better encourage your spouse's journey of faith?

Reflection

"Let no corrupting talk come out of your mouths, but only such as is good for building up, as fits the occasion, that it may give grace to those who hear."

— *Ephesians 4:29* —

Day 16 – Esteem

I will value you and your opinion.

> *"A fool takes no pleasure in understanding,
> but only in expressing his opinion."*
>
> — Proverbs 18:2 —

Esteem is not a word we often hear in our culture today. We tend to forget how to treat others with dignity and respect. Nowhere is this more true than in the marital covenant where God brings our respective strengths and weaknesses together. Opposites attract for a reason. As men and women, God uniquely created us to complement one another. That is why marriage is a beautiful picture of mutual dependance and collaboration. For we lean upon our spouse in good times and bad, lifting them up when life comes crashing down and celebrating life's blessings together.

Keep in mind, God exhorts us to appreciate and admire what makes us uniquely different as men and women. As such, we should treat one another with love and respect, for we are all equal heirs of the grace of God. Still, we get frustrated with our spouse because their perspective is different from our own. We fail to value one another's opinions because we are more concerned with asserting our own than hearing theirs. If only we would stop and listen, perhaps arguments would not be so common at home. The enemy wants us to think we know better, but our spouse compensates for our blind spots and guards us from thinking we always know best.

I can attest that Amber has helped me avoid sticking my foot in my mouth on countless occasions. She considers the emotional impact of her words before they are spoken, whereas I tend to bluntly state my opinion with little consideration for how it will be received. What I have learned is that filtering my thoughts through my wife is wise. She does not mother me in that I need her permission before saying anything. Rather, discerning my thoughts and feelings through her has helped me avoid digging a deeper hole for myself.

My esteem for Amber would not be possible without God revealing how precious she is to me. When we were first married, our opinions often clashed. We were both strong-willed and neither would relent our position. Fast-forward twenty-three years later, and I now understand that she has never tried to upstage me in our marriage. Instead, she has fulfilled the role God gave her to be my helper and counterbalance my weaknesses, to which there are many. Today, I appreciate her more than ever because I know that she makes up for areas of life where I am deficient. She completes me, per se, as I do for her as well.

Application

1. Which aspects of your spouse's character do you admire most?
2. How would you describe your spouse's value to your family? What makes them such a blessing?
3. Why is it easier to complain about your spouse's differing opinion than appreciate their unique point of view?
4. In what ways can you esteem your spouse more frequently?
5. How has your spouse esteemed you throughout your marriage?

Reflection

"Charm is deceitful, and beauty is vain, but a woman who fears the LORD is to be praised. Give her of the fruit of her hands and let her works praise her in the gates."

— *Proverbs 31:30–31* —

Day 17 – Communication

I will not shut you out.

"Know this, my beloved brothers: let every person be quick to hear, slow to speak, slow to anger; for the anger of man does not produce the righteousness of God."

— James 1:19–20 —

Communication can become a concern in our homes if we are not careful. When we attempt to win an argument rather than resolve a conflict, we demonstrate our spiritual maturity or lack thereof. Satan is always looking for an opportunity to create division and dissension in marriage. Therefore, we must guard our tongue and speak blessings into the heart of our spouse each day. However, there are times when we ice each other out and refuse to communicate. In those moments, our spouse is forced to guess what we are thinking and feeling because we have shut them out. It is never fair to assume we know what our spouse may be thinking. Rather, we are wise to ask good questions and listen to understand so we are not making false assumptions.

Verbal and nonverbal communication are critical to navigate trials in this world. We need accountability to protect us from harm because we cannot see our blind spots. It is one of the main reasons our spouse is God's greatest blessing to us. They tell us what we need to hear and console our heart when we are hurting. They speak truth into our mind and hold us close when we need to weep. They pick us up when we fall, speak encouraging words when we are frustrated, and remind us of who we are in Christ. In all things, communication is the linchpin of a vibrant and healthy marriage. We cannot survive without it, which means silencing our mate from speaking truth to us is unacceptable. If we desire a healthy marriage, we must keep the lines of communication open at all times to avoid giving the enemy a foothold to drive us apart.

There have been many instances where Amber and I have not been on the same page. Our words can easily get lost in translation, which is why we tend to over-communicate to ensure we fully understand what the other is thinking and feeling. The key for us is not defaulting into independent mode and inadvertently shutting one another out. Most of us want to have a say in how our family functions, and the worst thing we can do is silence each other's opinions or never ask for them. There have certainly been times in our marriage when I thought I was helping my wife by handling things on my own. Managing our budget was one of them. Amber would ask questions and I would interpret them as a lack of trust in what I was doing. What I learned was that her issue was not mistrust in me but a desire to know what is going on in the event something happened to me. In retrospect, I completely understand her dilemma. For as a recent heart attack survivor, her need for two-way communication is paramount in case something unfortunate were to ever happen to my health again.

Application

1. In what ways do you communicate well with your spouse?
2. How do you shut your spouse out by refusing to communicate?
3. Are most of your marital arguments due to poor communication or the issues themselves? How so?
4. What is one thing you can improve upon to communicate better?

Reflection

"A soft answer turns away wrath, but a harsh word stirs up anger. The tongue of the wise commends knowledge, but the mouths of fools pour out folly."

— *Proverbs 15:1–2* —

Day 18 – Wise Counsel

I will trust your advice.

> *"Blessed is the man who walks not in the counsel of the wicked, nor stands in the way of sinners, nor sits in the seat of scoffers; but his delight is in the law of the Lord, and on his law he meditates day and night. He is like a tree planted by streams of water that yields its fruit in its season, and its leaf does not wither. In all that he does, he prospers."*
>
> — Psalm 1:1–3 —

Discernment is a vital part of life. Every day we face decisions and knowing which path to take can be challenging if we lack truth to lead us. As Christians, we hold to the inerrancy and infallibility of Scripture, for it is as relevant today as ever before. When we struggle to discern God's will for our lives, we can read the Bible and gain wisdom to navigate the storms of life. However, there are times when we crave empathy and the comfort of a listening ear. It is not that we value the truth of God's Word any less. We simply want to purge our thoughts and make sense of our emotions.

Marriage should be our lifeline for personal communication with the one who knows us best. We should be able to trust that our spouse has our best interest in mind because they love us enough to tell us what we need to hear vs. what we desire. Appeasement has no place in conversations where wise counsel is critical. As such, we must not only seek our spouse's counsel to determine the wisest course of action but trust that their advice is Biblical. It is easy to make decisions without a care in the world for what anyone thinks, but that attitude is cancerous. For discernment begins and ends with Gospel truth, and our spouse can help point us to the true source of wisdom: Jesus Christ.

My wife is my best friend. Hands down, there is no one I go to for wise counsel other than her because she has my best interest in mind. Granted, she will hit me with hard truth if she feels I am drifting away from what Scripture teaches. Appeasement to spare my feelings is not in her vocabulary! I used to bristle at her unapologetic demeanor towards me, but over time I have grown to understand she loves so much that she would risk our relationship to ensure I do not sin.

In retrospect, I did not appreciate her stern words of warning years ago, but time has proven how wise she is despite my prideful heart. Rarely is she off-base because she knows me so well, and I praise God for blessing me with a wife who gives me sound advice from Scripture, even when it is presented more blunt and honest than I prefer. Not every husband has a wife who is strong in her faith, but Amber has saved me from countless pitfalls by offering solid wisdom and discernment. I do not know where my life would be without her and honestly, I do not care to consider it. She is my most trusted friend, and I am humbled to call her my bride and shoulder to cry upon when I need comfort and support.

Application

1. Whose wise counsel do you trust most? Why?
2. How has your spouse's counsel helped you make wise decisions?
3. What has caused you to doubt your spouse's counsel on occasion?
4. How can you ensure your counsel always aligns with God's Word?

Reflection

"Listen to advice and accept instruction, that you may gain wisdom in the future. Many are the plans in the mind of a man, but it is the purpose of the LORD that will stand."

— Proverbs 19:20–21 —

Day 19 – Accountability

I will heed your warnings.

"And we urge you, brothers, admonish the idle, encourage the fainthearted, help the weak, be patient with them all."

— 1 Thessalonians 5:14 —

Marriage is a tutorial on how to give and take in life. Reciprocity is important to show grace and mercy and receive it in return. Nowhere is this more evident than how we hold each other liable to the authority of Scripture. Accountability can be our greatest asset or most glaring deficiency. We can love it or hate it depending on our attitude and perspective. What we cannot deny is how desperately we need Biblical accountability to love our spouse like Jesus would. The challenge is we do not always want corrective advice on how to mold our character. Instead, we often bristle at the sound of criticism or lash out in anger rather than receive the counsel our spouse may provide.

What we must consider is that accountability is our spouse's way of protecting us. If we assume their intent is to harm, we will never listen or take their warnings to heart. The enemy wants us to interpret their advice as a blatant attack. He delights when we ignore wisdom because he wants us to make poor decisions based upon our feelings. In many ways, our ability to receive accountability is dependent upon trust. For if we do not trust our spouse's motives, their ability to guard our heart is severely limited. Speaking truth in love is the epitome of being held accountable when we are headed towards destruction. Thus, we should be thankful that our spouse is willing to protect us no matter the cost.

For example, I love to make people laugh. There is just something about brightening someone's day with a joke or pun which can break the ice in a room and help people feel more comfortable. Needless to say, I have learned that humor is best reserved when I take my audience into consideration. Nowhere is this more evident than in my interactions with other women, for it can be easy to come off as playful or flirtatious when it was not my intent. Needless to say, Amber picked up on that bad habit of mine early in our marriage and has brought it to my attention rather sternly on more than one occasion.

I remember balking at the idea that I was being flirtatious with other women by being funny. To me, I was just being myself. There was no harm in making others laugh but it bothered Amber nonetheless, and I quickly disregarded her concerns as being overly protective. However, the more I examined my heart's intention, the more convicted I felt that I was idolizing humor at the expense of my wife's heart and mind. Today, I am much more cautious of drawing attention to myself or cracking jokes when I am in the presence of other women. Some may think I am crazy and blowing it out of proportion, but Amber's peace of mind is the only thing I care about and I want to honor her accountability.

Application

1. Do you appreciate your spouse's accountability? Why or why not?
2. What must accountability look and feel like to truly be effective?
3. In what areas have you rejected your spouse's accountability?
4. How has your spouse's accountability protected you from harm?

Reflection

"Let the word of Christ dwell in you richly, teaching and admonishing one another in all wisdom, singing psalms and hymns and spiritual songs, with thankfulness in your hearts to God."

— Colossians 3:16 —

Day 20 – Understanding

I will respect your feelings.

"Let love be genuine. Abhor what is evil; hold fast to what is good. Love one another with brotherly affection. Outdo one another in showing honor."

— Romans 12:9–10 —

Emotions have a way of wreaking havoc on our minds. They can pull us in countless directions and make us assume things are true when clearly they are not. It goes without saying that Satan likes to play tricks on us. Our minds are his playground and he wants us to make decisions based on emotions instead of truth. As such, marital trust is important because we often lean on each other to validate how we are feeling in the moment. The challenge is striking a balance between indifference and accountability. Our spouse will tell us what we need to hear if we are willing to listen, but we can also be tempted to wash our hands of their counsel and not care at all if we are not careful.

The key to loving our spouse with understanding is by helping them filter their thoughts and feelings through God's Word. We can respect their emotions and the reality of their struggles, but we must gently point them to the Bible to validate fact from fiction. By doing so, we support them in their time of need but guard against adding fuel to the fire. We certainly empathize with their pain and sorrow because we are one flesh. What they feel, we feel, for love unites us. However, we must avoid standing by and watching them drive their minds into despair under the assumption that God is powerless to save. Instead, we must point them to the Lord as we guard their heart from the enemy.

Like most women, my wife has battled with cultural acceptance her entire life. Measuring up to the world's standard of fashion and beauty is a tireless endeavor. What once was considered the ideal look or body type can change quickly. Thus, measuring up to a moving target is no small feat. Making things worse are the body changes Amber has experienced through the years enduring five pregnancies, not to mention aging in general. In all ways, she tends to see herself from a glass-half-empty perspective, which breaks my heart because she is absolutely beautiful in my eyes.

I spend a lot of time affirming my wife because the world is ruthless in how it makes a woman feel so inadequate. I respect how Amber sees herself but in no way do I endorse self-deprecation either. I love her too much and refuse to let her believe anything other than the fact that she is perfectly made in the image of God. So while I respect how she feels about herself, I guard her mind from believing she is inadequate in any way. Are there things she would like to change about herself? Of course, but that has no bearing on how I see her as my beloved bride.

Application

1. How can you live with your spouse in a more understanding way?
2. What difference would it make if you began affirming your spouse based on who they are in Christ vs. the world's relative standards?
3. How can you begin to filter your thoughts and feelings through the absolute truth of God's Word more often?
4. Why must you be your spouse's biggest supporter and champion?

Reflection

"Yes, if you call out for insight and raise your voice for understanding, if you seek it like silver and search for it as for hidden treasures, then you will understand the fear of the LORD and find the knowledge of God."

— Proverbs 2:3–5 —

Day 21 – Prayer

I will pray with you and over you.

> *"Do not be anxious about anything, but in everything by prayer and supplication with thanksgiving let your requests be made known to God. And the peace of God, which surpasses all understanding, will guard your hearts and your minds in Christ Jesus."*
>
> — Philippians 4:6–7 —

If we had to pinpoint the greatest struggle in most marriages, prayer would be near the top of the list. It is one area of our lives which tends to be forgotten, not because it is inconsequential but because we fail to consistently make time to pray together as a married couple and family. Prayer is a common struggle for most Christ-followers. It is arguably the hardest spiritual discipline to master because it feels one-directional. However, God speaks to us through His Word. As such, if we are not studying Scripture daily and prioritizing 1-on-1 time with our heavenly Father, we will never see the fruit of our prayer discipline come to fruition.

Prayer is all about returning to center—mentally, emotionally, and spiritually. It allows us to purge our minds of all our random thoughts and feelings and lay them at the feet of Jesus. In marriage, it serves a dual purpose because it allows our spouse to know what is weighing heavy on our heart while we offer praise and supplication to God. It is an intimate moment we should not take for granted, yet we tend to avoid prayer or minimize it to sidestep vulnerability. The problem is that when we fail to come together in prayer, Satan is given ample opportunity to isolate our minds. Prayer is powerful because it sheds light into the darkness of our hearts and allows God to meet us in the valley. The real question is whether we will use it to strengthen our marital covenant or continue to minimize its importance.

Amber would attest that prayer has been a glaring weakness in our marriage. We rarely come together to pray as a couple, because I have been too lazy to make it a priority. I feel intimidated praying with her and struggle disciplining myself to pray alone too. It has always been a mental hurdle for me, but it will never improve unless I stop dwelling upon insecurities and lead as God expects. Amber needs me to lead our family in prayer—not just with her but our girls as well. In retrospect, God has taught me that corporate prayer is a missed opportunity to love my wife and share my heart with her. The Lord knows what I am thinking and feeling, but that does not mean Amber is on the same page unless I humble myself and let her in to enjoy spiritual intimacy together. Thankfully, I have begun leading prayer in our home and it has been powerful reading God's Word together and praying for one another as a family. Granted, we still struggle with consistency, but that is on me to not let distractions interfere with prayer.

Application

1. How often do you pray with your spouse? What excuses hold you back from praying together more frequently and consistently?
2. Which excuses do you use to justify your lack of personal prayer?
3. Why is it so powerful to hear your spouse praying aloud for you?
4. What impact would it have if your family gathered together daily to pray for one another?

Reflection

"Rejoice always, pray without ceasing, give thanks in all circumstances; for this is the will of God in Christ Jesus for you. Do not quench the Spirit."

— *1 Thessalonians 5:16–19* —

Day 22 – Worship

I will glorify the Lord with you.

"O LORD, you are my God; I will exalt you; I will praise your name, for you have done wonderful things, plans formed of old, faithful and sure."

— Isaiah 25:1 —

Worship is the epitome of the Christian life. God created us to have relationship with Him, and worship is our golden opportunity to thank the Lord for who He is and all He has done for us. We glorify our Father in heaven because He is worthy of praise. He is the giver of all good things, especially our spouse, for He made us to live in communion together. Oftentimes, we fail to see the blessings of life as a married couple. Without exception, our spouse should be our best friend because we have the opportunity to share every intimate detail of our lives together. That type of gift is what makes a marriage special as we gather to praise God for His sovereign provision. How then can we worship Him more by coming together as a family?

The Lord knows that we need our spouse to pray for us when we are downtrodden and worship with us in times of joy and sorrow. The key is worshipping Him no matter how we feel and interceding for one another in prayer. Not a day should go by that we do not praise God for our beloved despite their failures, for they endure our sinful actions as well. If anything, imperfections magnify our need to praise the Lord in good times and in bad and despite how we may feel in the moment. Worshipping Jesus is not a cross we bear but the greatest honor and privilege of our lives. It is our daily opportunity to humble ourselves and thank Him for all He has done for us. Families who worship God together realize the importance of giving thanks as one heart and mind. It unites our hearts and gives us greater appreciation for who God is.

Corporate worship as a family is a mixed bag for us. We worship the Lord together on Sundays with the body of Christ, but we do not have a specified time where we sing praises to Him at home. We certainly have gospel conversations each day and speak truth in love to each other, but taking time to worship God for who He is does not happen as often as it should. We listen to worship music daily yet often fail to lift our voices up in unison together like we do on Sundays mornings. What I have learned is that taking time to thank and praise God daily is critical to the health of our home. When we stop and talk about who God is, what He has done, and all we have graciously been given, praise pours out. That does not mean we have to sing collectively, per se, but our intent is to ensure that we do not take the Lord for granted. He is worthy to be praised and we can strengthen our family bond more by worshipping Him together each day, both in song and through our conversations with each other.

Application

1. Who is God to you? What about Him compels you to give thanks and praise for all He has done in your life?
2. Why is worshipping together as a family so important?
3. How can you incorporate praise and worship into your home?
4. What would you like to praise God for concerning your spouse? What difference would it make if they overheard you telling Him?

Reflection

"Oh come, let us worship and bow down; let us kneel before the LORD, our Maker! For he is our God, and we are the people of his pasture, and the sheep of his hand."

— Psalm 95:6–7 —

Day 23 – Ministry

I will serve others alongside you.

"As each has received a gift, use it to serve one another, as good stewards of God's varied grace: whoever speaks, as one who speaks oracles of God; whoever serves, as one who serves by the strength that God supplies—in order that in everything God may be glorified through Jesus Christ."

— *1 Peter 4:10–11* —

Serving alongside one another is one of the most rewarding aspects of ministry because we get to share the love of Jesus in a real and tangible way. There is something extra special, though, about serving the Lord with our spouse as opposed to separately. It reminds us that as we both pursue Christ, we grow closer together because our end goal is mutual. Volunteering is an exercise in humbling ourselves to meet the needs of those around us. There are several opportunities within our churches and communities to bless others, but serving as one is extra special because we get to witness the Spirit working in and through our spouse to the glory of Jesus' name.

Doing ministry together is also an extension of quality time for a marriage. Of course, date nights are fun, but serving together allows us to see the compassion and empathy of our beloved firsthand. It affirms the quality of their character and reminds us of how blessed we are to enjoy life together as husband and wife. As such, it is critical we are unified in spirit and truth so Christ is glorified in all we say and do. The more we lock arms and love others sacrificially, the deeper our spiritual intimacy will grow as we pursue Christ as a married couple. Ministry is not something we do but who we are as Christians. Therefore, let us take every thought captive and consider our time with intentionality and purpose as we love and serve those God has uniquely placed in our path each day.

Amber and I love shepherding men's and women's discipleship groups. The opportunity to pay forward all God has taught us in our lives and marriage is a unique blessing. Amber leads women on Monday nights at our church and I lead men on Tuesday nights. However, we have also come together and led teen groups as well on occasion. Granted, we are still in separate rooms, but it allows us to use our gifts of shepherding and discipleship to impact the next generation.

The key was finding an area of need in our church where our spiritual gifts aligned with serving together. We love discipleship. It is our greatest passion along with Biblical counseling, so it made sense for us to serve the body of Christ in a way that merged our gifts with a need we could help solve together. It has allowed us to invest in the lives of youth while also worshipping God together through volunteering our time and energy for His kingdom. It is a time investment but also incredibly rewarding because we get to serve alongside one another.

Application

1. Do you minister together as a couple? Why or why not?
2. How have you found creative ways to serve the Lord together? If not, where could you align your spiritual gifts to meet a local need?
3. What are the benefits of serving together as opposed to separately?
4. How has God blessed your marriage by ministering together? How does it make you feel watching your spouse love and serve others?

Reflection

*"For you were called to freedom, brothers.
Only do not use your freedom as an opportunity for the flesh,
but through love serve one another."*

— *Galatians 5:13* —

Day 24 – Gifts

I will encourage your spiritual gifts.

> "Having gifts that differ according to the grace given to us, let us use them: if prophecy, in proportion to our faith; if service, in our serving; the one who teaches, in his teaching; the one who exhorts, in his exhortation; the one who contributes, in generosity; the one who leads, with zeal; the one who does acts of mercy, with cheerfulness."
>
> — Romans 12:6–8 —

We are all unique. There is not another person in the world who is exactly like us because God made us different for a reason. As Paul wrote, the portion of grace He bestows on us differs from one individual to another, so we are not performing the same function in His kingdom but serving different purposes. Whether it be prophesy, service, teaching, exhortation, generosity, acts of mercy, or other gifts, God has given His children the ability to do things which far surpass their natural abilities and talents. Spiritual gifts are intended to minister to those around us and point them to the saving grace of Jesus Christ. They are unique and meant to bless others. Therefore, it is critical we champion our spouse's gifts and encourage their efforts.

The amazing thing about spiritual gifts is that the Lord allows us to play a unique part in His redemptive plan of salvation throughout the world. The challenge is we are often too busy to utilize our spiritual gifts and feel unfulfilled when they remain dormant. However, that is where we can love our spouse by championing them to use their gifts and providing the time needed to make it happen. God has blessed us with unique gifts for a specific purpose, and it is our job to not only utilize what He has graciously given us but support our spouse as they discover the plan He has for them to minister to others as well.

Over the years, I have seen God use Amber in mighty ways for His glory.

Her ability to provide wisdom and counsel to women who are struggling has been tremendous. She has the unique ability to feel the pain of others and empathize with their suffering. We often joke in our home that Amber can cry at a moment's notice. She just feels emotion more intimately than anyone I have ever known, and it is powerful to see her use her gift of compassion to minister to other women.

Because her heart is so tender and she invests as much time as needed ministering to others, she has earned the trust of countless women through the years. Her counsel is always Biblical and her empathy lets others know that the wisdom she shares is for their benefit. I have never met anyone with a bigger heart than my wife, and it is beautiful to see her invest in the lives of other women by discipling their minds and shepherding their hearts. Nothing gives me greater joy than watching her utilize her gifts for God's glory. It energizes her soul and allows her to pay forward the grace and mercy of Jesus Christ to others.

Application

1. What are your spouse's spiritual gifts? Do you know? If not, why?
2. How can you encourage your spouse to use their spiritual gifts?
3. How are your spiritual gifts different from your spouse?
4. What changes could you make to your personal schedule so that your spouse can invest more time utilizing their giftedness?
5. How have your spouse's spiritual gifts been a blessing to you?

Reflection

"Now there are varieties of gifts, but the same Spirit; and there are varieties of service, but the same Lord; and there are varieties of activities, but it is the same God who empowers them all in everyone."

— 1 Corinthians 12:4–6 —

Day 25 – Holiness

I will celebrate the changes you make.

"Do not be conformed to this world, but be transformed by the renewal of your mind, that by testing you may discern what is the will of God, what is good and acceptable and perfect."

— Romans 12:2 —

Life is full of choices. We can choose to follow Christ or reject Him altogether; humble ourselves or remain steadfast in defiant pride. We must not merely recognize areas where we need to change but make the effort to chart our course and pursue holiness. The key is leveraging intentionality, determination, and consistency to our benefit, and our spouse can play a pivotal role helping us achieve that goal. There is nothing more powerful than positive affirmation from loved ones. Their belief in our ability to change and encouragement to do so are powerful tools of motivation. They help us celebrate victories as we allow the Lord to mold and refine our character.

Ambition can be powerful if channeled toward sanctification and becoming a more devoted follower of Jesus Christ. However, if the changes our spouse makes benefits their faith journey, we should not only encourage them but celebrate their progress. Change is often a 2-steps-forward, 1-step-back process. Adversity and trials are bound to arise as we modify our thoughts and behavior. Thus, it is critical we support each other as we identify areas which lack holiness and begin overhauling our heart and mind. We must pray for one another and champion our respective efforts to become more like Jesus. For Satan does not want us to succeed, and we are wise to guard against him.

As a homeschool family of six, quiet times are difficult to come by. Our kids are always with us, so finding a designated time and place to spend quality time with the Lord is easier said than done. Regardless, I know that Amber needs time each day to read her Bible and pray, so we strategically build in quiet time for her each morning. Granted, not every day is perfect, but most days she has uninterrupted time reserved to spend with God however she pleases.

What I appreciate is her dedication to read the Bible and pray daily. She knows that she needs wisdom to be the wife and mother God calls her to be, so it is top priority. It helps focus her attention on holiness and gives her peace of mind to start the day. Our entire family benefits when Amber has quiet time with the Lord, so we ensure she gets it with minimal distractions as possible. Quiet time was not always a part of her daily routine. However, the older she gets, the more she realizes how much she needs the Lord daily. She enjoys spending time with Him, so it is imperative I help protect that time slot so she can pursue holiness.

Application

1. Are you your spouse's biggest cheerleader? Why or why not?
2. Why is it important to champion the positive changes your spouse has made in their journey of faith?
3. How has your spouse encouraged you by their pursuit of holiness?
4. In what areas of life do you need to pursue holiness more to grow closer with Christ?

Reflection

"As obedient children, do not be conformed to the passions of your former ignorance, but as he who called you is holy, you also be holy in all your conduct, since it is written, 'You shall be holy, for I am holy.'"

— 1 Peter 1:14–16 —

Day 26 – Empathy

I will identify with your struggles.

"Rejoice with those who rejoice, weep with those who weep."
— Romans 12:15 —

The ability to empathize with another person is one of life's greatest treasures. Whether we have been on the receiving end or the one administering it, empathy is a precious gift, especially in marriage. It means that we identify with the cries of their heart, not necessarily what they are struggling with specifically. We can weep and mourn with them because we are both partakers of God's unending grace and mercy. While empathy often comes more easily to wives, it does not mean husbands cannot learn how to meet them in the valley of despair. All that is required is a heart willing to be vulnerable and shoulder one another's burdens when they cannot bear them any longer.

Scripture reminds us that weeping and rejoicing are a part of life. We often forget that joy and trials go hand-in-hand in the big picture of God's sovereignty (Jam. 1:2). What we endure on this side of heaven is meant to sanctify our character and mold us into the image of Christ. In turn, we look for the silver-lining of God's grace amid our hardships which give meaning to what He has in store to teach us. It is difficult, though, to focus our eyes on the horizon when we feel all alone in the valley. We may know there is light at the end of the tunnel, but we also need our spouse to empathize with how we feel. The enemy preys upon those who have no one to lean on in times of trial, so we must ensure our spouse knows that we feel their pain every step of the way.

We are blessed with four amazing girls, but there was a time when it did not seem to be God's plan. After the birth of our second daughter, Amber had trouble getting pregnant again. We knew her hormones had become erratic following her last pregnancy, but we did not expect she would be barren for almost eight years before God miraculously reopened her womb unexpectedly.

That season of time was extremely difficult. Depression was a real struggle despite my best efforts to comfort my wife. Not until the end of that period did we discover what was inevitably causing the issue. I remember feeling pretty inept not knowing how to help Amber overcome sorrow. At the time, she was in mourning, and it took many years until she finally came to terms that more children seemed to not be in God's plan for us. I would love to say that I helped her find peace in the storm, but it was the Lord who gave her strength to overcome her depression. All I did was empathize with her emotions and encouraged her to vent her thoughts and feelings. Inevitably, God did reopen her womb again which led to three more miraculous pregnancies. Praise the Lord!

Application

1. What must empathy look like to be helpful and effective?
2. Give an example where empathy was required to help your spouse overcome a deep personal struggle. What did you learn as a result?
3. How has empathy enhanced spiritual intimacy in your marriage?
4. How has a lack of empathy from you made your spouse feel alone and isolated?

Reflection

"This is my commandment, that you love one another as I have loved you. Greater love has no one than this, that someone lay down his life for his friends."

— John 15:12–13 —

Day 27 – Compassion

I will help you cope with trials.

> *"Blessed be the God and Father of our Lord Jesus Christ, the Father of mercies and God of all comfort, who comforts us in all our affliction, so that we may be able to comfort those who are in any affliction, with the comfort with which we ourselves are comforted by God."*
>
> — 2 Corinthians 1:3–4 —

Compassion and empathy are a package deal. We cannot presume to have compassion if we have no empathy for how someone is thinking and feeling. Both attributes involve living with our spouse in an understanding way, but compassion goes one step further to meet a need vs. simply empathizing with thoughts and emotions. Showing compassion was the epitome of Jesus' ministry. No matter where He traveled, crowds flocked to Him because they knew He not only had empathy for their sad plight but a willingness to show compassion. It should make us consider whether or not we merely empathize with our spouse in their hour of need or go above and beyond the call of duty to do whatever it takes to alleviate their burdens.

Being compassionate allows our spouse to witness how much we love them in real and tangible ways. Satan often tempts us to doubt whether we care about each other in our hour of need. He wants us to fear that our love for each other is conditional rather than selfless. For if we believe we are all alone, we may not recognize our spouse's love when they attempt to help us. Trials have a unique ability to bind our hearts with despair if we allow. As such, we must ensure our spouse knows that we will lift them up from the ashes by stepping into the gap and shielding them from the enemy's schemes. Compassion is critical to a healthy marriage because we shoulder each other's burdens, pointing them to Christ and walking with them every step of the way.

Roughly six months into our marriage, my Mom was diagnosed with ovarian cancer. She fought hard for eighteen months undergoing chemotherapy treatments, but the cancer spread and it was evident she would not live much longer heading into Christmas, 2003. We had just moved from Indiana to Maryland at that time, but Amber was determined to help despite my mother living in Michigan. Filled with compassion, she decided to move in with my parents and help take of my Mom, 24/7, along with my Mom's best friend who also moved in to help. Over the course of a month, they maximized quality time together and handled all her medical needs to alleviate the pressure from my Dad's plate. In the end, they spent quality time taking care of her until she passed away at home. Never before had I seen compassion on display like that, but those memories are forever etched in my mind as an example of what it means to love like Jesus would and show selfless love and compassion to those in need.

Application

1. Why is compassion so critical to a healthy marriage?
2. How is your spouse more empathetic towards you when you long for compassion instead?
3. In what ways can you be more compassionate with your spouse?
4. How has your spouse's compassion been a blessing to you in your hour of need?

Reflection

"But if anyone has the world's goods and sees his brother in need, yet closes his heart against him, how does God's love abide in him? Little children, let us not love in word or talk but in deed and in truth."

— 1 John 3:17–18 —

Day 28 – Humor

I will cheer you up with laughter.

"A joyful heart is good medicine, but a crushed spirit dries up the bones."
— *Proverbs 17:22* —

Laughter is good medicine because it can change our outlook and improve our negative attitude. The ability to laugh at days to come reminds us that we need not worry about tomorrow because God is in complete control. Anxiety has the potential to consume our hearts and minds, if we are not careful, which is why we must take each day in stride and not worry about the future. In many ways, humor has the power to change our perspective. For when nothing seems to go our way, simply laughing can be the difference between losing our mind and putting stress behind us. That does not mean all our problems will magically go away, but laughter allows us to cope with pain and count our trials as joy when life becomes too difficult to bear.

Humor can also help us enjoy life. It is a relational tool that allows us to have common ground with our mate as we celebrate life together. Laughter lifts our spirits and brings a smile to our face, which we often need when feeling overwhelmed. There is nothing more therapeutic to a marriage than joking, laughing, and enjoying quality time together. Too often, we forget the importance of being playful and lighthearted with our spouse. Time goes by quickly and the laughs we shared during the early years can become a distant memory. Thus, maintaining a good sense of humor and having fun as we age is important. Life will overrun us with reasons to stress and worry, but laughter counterbalances worry by reminding us that life is short and to take each day in stride.

I love to make Amber laugh because she has one of the sweetest laughs I have ever heard. Once anyone hears her laugh, in turn, they do as well because hers is infectious. When we were dating, I would do anything I could to make her laugh. I believe she would say that my sense of humor was her favorite thing about me back then. Our relationship was long-distance, so all we did was talk on the phone and laugh for hours on end.

I treasure those memories because laughter has been an integral part of our marriage ever since. We enjoy comedy shows and funny movies, but our tastes have changed as we have matured spiritually. We do not enjoy crude humor like we once did. Now, we take life in stride because there are plenty of things to laugh about when we stop and smell the roses. Being a parent provides opportunities each day to store up memories for a later date and laugh about. No matter what season of life we have found ourselves in, being able to laugh together has saved our marriage in many ways. It has been much-needed medicine and enabled us to enjoy quality time together, just like we did many years ago when we first met.

Application

1. What are some of your favorite funny memories as a couple?
2. In what ways have you lost the joy of laughter in your home?
3. Give an example where laughter has been good medicine for your marriage and family?
4. Do you believe God has a sense of humor? Why or why not?

Reflection

"Go your way. Eat the fat and drink sweet wine and send portions to anyone who has nothing ready, for this day is holy to our Lord. And do not be grieved, for the joy of the LORD is your strength."

— Nehemiah 8:10 —

Day 29 – Connection

I will make quality time for you.

"But do not overlook this one fact, beloved, that with the Lord one day is as a thousand years, and a thousand years as one day."

— 2 Peter 3:8 —

How different would our life look if we knew how much time we had left before we died? Would we worry less and enjoy life more? What impact would it have on the quality of time we spend with our spouse? Would we waste our days arguing over trivial pursuits or reconcile conflict quickly to enjoy peace and happiness? In many ways, quality time is all about perspective. Tomorrow is not guaranteed, yet we assume that we can resolve conflict later or tell our loved ones how much they mean to us when we see them again. The problem is that if we do not make the most of what God has given us, we will one day live with regret for not appreciating what we had in the first place.

Connection is all about spending time together. It would be difficult for a marriage to survive long distance for an indefinite amount of time. We need face-to-face interaction with our spouse to connect as one—physically, mentally, emotionally, and spiritually. For example, military families understand the value of quality time better than anyone else, because their ability to connect as one is severely challenged. They would sacrifice anything for the hours we get to spend with our spouse every day, so why do we not appreciate quality time more? Keep in mind, healthy marriages praise and thank the Lord for the opportunity to enjoy time together. For today may be our last, and we are wise to make the most of it before it is too late.

Amber and I met online back before dating apps became popular. Neither of us were looking for a relationship. We simply met in a chat room on Yahoo and the rest is history. However, long distance was a challenge because we lived about 600-miles away. We did drive and fly to see each other a few times, but that was relatively minimal over the course of our dating. What we did have were phones, so we used them to our advantage back when long-distance calls were free on nights and weekends!

In total, we dated for 5-months, got engaged, and married 3-months later. We spoke every night when we were not together and connected easily despite the distance. Still, it was not the same as being local to each other. We missed out on what most couples take for granted, so it was a shell shock going from talking only on the phone each day to living together as husband and wife. It took a while for us to get the hang of it, but over time we learned from each other and our connection grew. Today, we see each other all day, every day, since I work from home and Amber homeschools. Most couples could not do what we do, but we would not have it any other way because God has truly made us one flesh in heart, mind, and soul.

Application

1. What does quality time look like from your spouse's perspective?
2. How and when do you typically enjoy quality time together?
3. What changes can you make to connect more with your spouse?
4. Why is it important to connect spiritually as a married couple?

Reflection

"For everything there is a season, and a time for every matter under heaven: a time to be born, and a time to die; a time to plant, and a time to pluck up what is planted."

— *Ecclesiastes 3:1–2* —

Day 30 – Peace

I will resolve conflict quickly with you.

"Be angry and do not sin; do not let the sun go down on your anger and give no opportunity to the devil."

— Ephesians 4:26–27 —

How often do we let the sun go down on anger in marriage? When conflict arises in the home and we are faced with reconciling our differences, the desire to walk away and deal with it later often feels like the best option. In some cases, it may be. However, if we chose to stop arguing and start working together, we could resolve conflict today and not put it off until tomorrow. Keep in mind, winning an argument is meaningless. Why would we aim for victory and defeat our spouse? This mentality will only drive a wedge in our relationship and create dominating thoughts. Many marriages have ended in divorce because couples could not achieve peace in the home. Therefore, we are wise to learn how to be peacemakers and resolve conflicts quickly.

Oftentimes, we are too busy fighting to see the forest through the trees. We would rather exhaust ourselves in a war of words than filter our emotions and fix our issues. Arguing solves nothing. It merely destroys our unconditional love and respect for one another. That is why we must not allow conflict to fester but resolve our differences quickly to ensure peace is maintained in the home. In fairness, not every conflict can be resolved immediately, nor should we appease our mate to avoid a disagreement. However, tension can always be diffused by praying together and asking God to grant us wisdom, discernment, understanding, and patience. Conflict is a part of every marriage but learning how to effectively deal with it is the key to achieving peace.

One thing Amber and I quickly learned when we got married was that our conflict resolution styles were completely different. I wanted to resolve issues now, whereas she preferred to think on them for a while and discuss them later. She also has a phenomenal memory, while mine is terrible, so waiting to talk played into my forgetfulness.

It took us a while to find a rhythm, but we learned how to resolve some issues quickly while letting others simmer, as needed. We certainly try to avoid going to bed angry, but we are more concerned about not letting disagreements disrupt the peace in our home than anything else. That is one reason why we tend to resolve conflict in the public areas of our home rather than behind closed doors. Granted, some issues cannot be addressed in front of our girls, but we address most publicly so they can learn how to resolve differences of opinion lovingly and respectfully. Not every conflict is handled perfectly, but we ensure that no issue is big enough to drive a wedge of dissension into our home or marriage.

Application

1. Is peace a pearl of great prize in your marriage? Why or why not?
2. How do you work well together to resolve conflict in your home?
3. What bad habits do you need to break in your conflict resolution?
4. What are your respective conflict resolution styles in marriage? Do you resolve most issues quickly or sleep on them? How so?

Reflection

"Repay no one evil for evil but give thought to do what is honorable in the sight of all. If possible, so far as it depends on you, live peaceably with all."

— Romans 12:17–18 —

Day 31 – In-Laws

I will love your family as my own.

> *"Therefore a man shall leave his father and his mother and hold fast to his wife, and they shall become one flesh."*
>
> — *Genesis 2:24* —

When a husband and wife make a covenantal commitment to one another in holy matrimony, not only are two hearts made one but two families are brought together as well. However, while we get to pick and choose our spouse, we are not given the same privilege concerning their respective family. It is a package deal which can play a key role in bringing a marriage closer together or driving us further apart. Keep in mind, none of us were given the opportunity to choose our parents nor the extended family we share. We are simply expected to honor our father and mother as God commands which includes our in-laws when we get married.

When it comes to blending two families together, grace and mercy are required. Maintaining balance is key to ensure we are not favoring one family over the other or causing dissension at holiday times. It is also important, though, to make decisions in the best interest of the family we create and ensure our covenant is protected. Many couples struggle to find a happy medium while trying to appease both families, but the key is ensuring we are one heart and mind as husband and wife to ensure our message is consistent with each family. It helps to diffuse tension as we decide what is best for own family unit.

I'll be the first to admit that it took me a while to gel with my in-laws, but I had to mature as well and realize that my job as a man was to not only take care of Amber and our girls but her parents as well. As a write this devotional, we only have one parent still living. Both of my parents have passed away as well as Amber's

Dad, so her Mom is the only living grandparent for our girls to spend time with. That knowledge changes things. It also puts a spotlight on the need for me to step up and help take care of my mother-in-law as the Bible teaches regarding widows.

For many years, there was a bit of tension is my relationship with Amber's mom. We are different people, but I have learned to appreciate who she is and her unique way of expressing love through gifts and acts of service. I grew up in a very touchy-feely, words of affirmation culture, but that is not how Amber was raised. I used to get frustrated by that, but time has shown me that love can be expressed in different ways. Amber's Mom has been played a unique role in the upbringing of our girls and I am thankful she has always been there for every play, recital, or competition to love and support them. Are we still very different people? Of course. However, as time goes by, I see far more similarities between us than differences because we share what is most important in common: our love for Jesus and our love for Amber.

Application

1. How are your respective families different? How are they similar?
2. What is one way you can love your spouse's family better?
3. Why is balance so important to keep peace between your families?
4. What aspect of your spouse's upbringing do you appreciate most?
5. Are you ready and willing to be a caregiver for your spouse's father or mother one day, if necessary? Why or why not?

Reflection

"Honor your father and your mother, as the LORD your God commanded you, that your days may be long, and that it may go well with you in the land that the LORD your God is giving you."

— *Deuteronomy 5:16* —

Day 32 – Respect

I will teach our children to honor you.

> *"She looks well to the ways of her household and does not eat the bread of idleness. Her children rise up and call her blessed; her husband also, and he praises her: 'Many women have done excellently, but you surpass them all.'"*
>
> — Proverbs 31:27–29 —

Respect is foundational to any healthy relationship. We can debate whether it should be given or earned, but we cannot ignore its importance in the home and beyond. Respect communicates that we value who someone is and where they come from. Nowhere is this more evident than in the home. Mutual love and respect between a husband and wife are central to modeling righteous behavior for our children, especially in the early years. Case in point: if a child is taught why respect is important, what it looks like, and how to apply it, they will set themselves up for success and be worthy of respect as well.

Conversely, our example of disrespect can have grave consequences based on how we talk to each other. If we demean, belittle, argue, or rebel, we ultimately communicate a lack of respect. There is no honor associated with being critical or tearing others down, so we must be careful with our words and teach our children to respect our spouse unconditionally. That does not mean our mate must be perfect to warrant respect. It simply means that we teach them respect for authority because the Bible instructs us to honor our father and our mother. For we set the tone in speaking blessing, not cursing, over our loves ones to avoid coming across as hypocritical to our children.

Respect is important in our home. We do not allow backtalk of any kind to fester, especially from our girls. The challenge is that we are not perfect and speak harshly with each other in front of our girls at times. It does not happen often, but it has certainly forced me to take my lumps and own my hypocrisy when I model poor speech and foolish behavior. If I do not bridle my tongue and think before I speak, I can easily plant seeds of dissension in our home.

There is a distinct difference between receiving respect and being worthy of it. Scripture is clear that mothers and fathers are to be shown honor because of their authority position. However, it is far easier for my family to respect me if my behavior honors the Lord in everything I say and do. Similarly, my girls will respect their mother if I speak to Amber with kindness and gentleness. Thus, it is critical that I set the tone in my home by honoring their mother unconditionally. Thankfully, we have not had any major issues with our girls disrespecting my wife. There have been times when they have asserted their independence, but they have always revered their mother for the position God gave her in our home.

Application

1. How do you show honor and respect for your spouse?
2. In what ways do you need to be more respectful of your spouse?
3. What behavioral issues are you experiencing in your home that are due to your poor example? How so?
4. How can you speak more blessing than cursing to your spouse?

Reflection

"Children, obey your parents in the Lord, for this is right. Fathers, do not provoke your children to anger, but bring them up in the discipline and instruction of the Lord."

— *Ephesians 6:1,4* —

Day 33 – Unity

I will ensure we are on the same page.

"Finally, all of you, have unity of mind, sympathy, brotherly love, a tender heart, and a humble mind."

— 1 Peter 3:8 —

Unity is one of the defining characteristics of a healthy marriage. We will never agree on everything, but we must be willing to lay down our preferences to maintain peace in the home. Unity is all about keeping wedges of dissension from dividing our relationships. It forces us to compromise by separating needs from wants and challenges us to evaluate whether the hill we are willing to die on is worth it. It also guards us from manipulative tactics orchestrated by Satan to pit us against one another. The key is ensuring we are not unequally yoked in our faith (2 Cor. 6:14) so our standard of truth is the same. God's Word must be our common thread as we make decisions which impact our family. This helps us maintain unity and keeps the true enemy in our line of sight at all times: Satan.

In order to protect our family, we must have unity on major issues. Concerns such as religious beliefs, spending habits, parenting styles, conflict resolution tactics, and social influences are just a few topics that can wreak havoc in our relationships. Areas where we have drastic differences of opinion are a concern, but not all issues are equal in severity. What we decide to eat for dinner is trivial compared to living beyond our finances. Keep in mind, culture teaches us to embrace individuality, but that does not work in areas where we must be unified to protect our family from harm. Satan will easily exploit areas where we are miles apart to plant seeds of doubt and tempt us to think we are incompatible and better off walking away from our marriage.

Unity has easily been one of the greatest blessings Amber and I have in our marriage. We disagree at times and debate issues all the time, but we try to come together on hot topics which can have big consequences if do not take them seriously. This has allowed us to fight much less and focus on living for righteousness in our personal behavior. For example, my wife has always been a thrifty shopper. She loves yard sales and buys household items at them when it makes sense. Does that mean we never buy anything new? No, it doesn't, but we do try to be wise with our money in every way. We drink water at restaurants unless the drink is included. We do not waste money on alcohol or nicotine to have a good time. We developed more in-home dates when our girls were young to save on babysitting. All this to say, we have tried to stretch our money as far as possible and that has allowed us to be less anxious on finances than most couples. Certainly, we still disagree at times, but we strive toward unity for the sake of our marital health.

Application

1. How do you come to consensus in marriage when you disagree?
2. How has God blessed your unity on important marital concerns?
3. Give an example of an area where you are unified and one you are not. What has God taught you through both experiences?
4. How has your unity as a couple positively impacted your children?

Reflection

"I appeal to you, brothers, by the name of our Lord Jesus Christ, that all of you agree, and that there be no divisions among you, but that you be united in the same mind and the same judgment."

— 1 Corinthians 1:10 —

Day 34 – Trust

I will give you the benefit of the doubt.

"But above all, my brothers, do not swear, either by heaven or by earth or by any other oath, but let your 'yes' be yes and your 'no' be no, so that you may not fall under condemnation."

— James 5:12 —

Trust is a foundational pillar of any successful marriage. It gives our spouse peace of mind knowing that our word is fully dependable. Trust is built through consistency over time. It is steady and reliable. Each time we follow through on our commitments, we build trust; just as every time we tell the truth, we gain credibility. Trust is a byproduct of ethical behavior which means our personal character matters. We cannot demand that trust be given to us because past behavior dictates what people think about us today. If we have been true to our word, trust will be freely given. If not, then we have much work to do building a consistent pattern of behavior to change their opinion.

Conversely, distrust is magnified when we make empty promises. For example, if we commit to be somewhere or do something yet fail to follow through, it calls our integrity into question and makes others wonder if we can be completely trusted. How then can our spouse depend on us if we say one thing but do the exact opposite? Do we not see the direct correlation between our words and actions? Granted, none of us are perfect. We all make poor choices from time to time. However, if we expect to be given the benefit of the doubt by our spouse, we must give it freely in return as well. The challenge is that small things add up over time in the crucible of marriage. We tend to keep score and choose what we want to believe instead of trusting our spouse unconditionally. Thus, it is imperative we give our spouse the benefit of the doubt to avoid further tension in the home.

In twenty-three years of marriage, Amber and I have had our share of struggles around this issue. I went from being a trustworthy husband to losing all credibility overnight. Granted, I have spent many years rebuilding trust with my wife, but the aftermath of past sins can be hard to overcome. Amber forgave me, but forgetting is not in her DNA. As such, she has questioned my decision-making across all areas of my life, including financial decisions, driving habits, and how I behave around other women when she is not present. She has to remind herself that though I am not perfect, I'm not who I used to be and she can trust the changes I have made to my personal character. What I have learned is that consistency is key. I would likely not be married today if I did not make drastic changes in my life and stick to them. Has the road to redemption been easy? Absolutely not. There will always be a shred of doubt in the back of my wife's mind. That is a consequence of my actions which I humbly accept, but it does not define who I am today either. I cannot change the past, but I can live each day with integrity in gratitude to the one who died to set me free from sin: Jesus Christ—for only because of Him can I be trusted again.

Application

1. Why is trust beneficial to measure the health of your marriage?
2. Do you consider yourself trustworthy? Why or why not?
3. Which past sins have caused your spouse to doubt your credibility? How has that impacted your marriage today?
4. In what areas are you withholding trust from your spouse? Why?

Reflection

"One who is faithful in a very little is also faithful in much, and one who is dishonest in a very little is also dishonest in much."

— Luke 16:10 —

Day 35 – Privacy

I will ensure you hear things first.

> *"The words of a whisperer are like delicious morsels; they go down into the inner parts of the body."*
>
> — Proverbs 18:8 —

It is critically important to always maintain privacy in marriage. The intimate details we share together are for our spouse's ears only, that is unless we both choose to divulge our own personal details after-the-fact. Trust can easily be broken the minute we make what is private public. In turn, we must ensure our marital boundaries are firm to avoid sharing details about our spouse without their consent. Where things can get messy is seeking input from parents, siblings, or best friends without their permission. We assume that because we trust certain people, our friends and family are privy to knowledge which is exclusively private. Unfortunately, we undermine our spouse's faith in us when we break their trust and air their dirty laundry publicly.

Another area where many couples struggle is by talking to others before first consulting their spouse. There is nothing more bothersome than receiving information after-the-fact. It calls into question whether our spouse values our opinion over others and wants to hear what we have to say. Many times, it is easier to get opinions from an outside source as additional feedback can be helpful. However, consulting others first undermines the true intimacy of a marriage covenant. As such, if we want our spouse to be our most trusted confidante, then we must ensure all personal information is shared with them before anyone else and kept private unless they allow us to share it publicly.

I can remember having many conflicts on this issue when we were first married. Keep in mind, I uprooted my wife from the only home she ever knew and transported her many states away. She hardly knew anyone, started a new job, and had to figure out how to be married. Everything was different, so she often called home to talk to her Mom. It was understandable, all things considered. She longed for counsel and familiarity from the one she trusted her whole life. At first, it was not a big deal, but I began hearing things after Amber spoke to her Mom which bothered me.

Needless to say, I was a bit frustrated. She did not intend to be malicious in any way. She hadn't even noticed that I was hearing things for the first time after she had spoken to her Mom. She was just struggling to survive and I became overly sensitive assuming that the privacy of our marriage included a third party. It took many conversations to eventually reconcile the issue. We had become one flesh when we were married, but our hearts, minds, and souls were united when we forsook all others. It took time to iron out the wrinkles, but we now talk to each other first on practically everything which fosters incredible oneness and spiritual intimacy in our marriage covenant.

Application

1. Which areas of your marriage do you consider private? Why?
2. How has your spouse's discretion and protection over personal information you share been such a blessing?
3. Are there any viable reasons to not share intimate information with your spouse before talking to anyone else?
4. How can maintaining privacy enhance intimacy in your marriage?

Reflection

"Drink water from your own cistern, flowing water from your own well. Should your springs be scattered abroad, streams of water in the streets?"

— Proverbs 5:15–16 —

Day 36 – Liability

I will own the consequences of my actions.

"For we must all appear before the judgment seat of Christ, so that each one may receive what is due for what he has done in the body, whether good or evil."

— 2 Corinthians 5:10 —

One of the hardest lessons to learn in life is accepting complete responsibility for the consequences of our actions. Ownership is paramount to spiritual maturity. It demonstrates that we understand how our actions impact others and how willing we are to make amends for wrongs we have done. Liability is not a word we often think about in the context of marriage, but it is hypercritical to conflict resolution and repentance. In other words, we cannot expect to move on from the collateral damage of our foolish behavior if we justify our sins, minimize consequences, or blame shift responsibility.

As husbands and wives, we must set a godly example by modeling accountability in the home. There is a price to be paid for every selfish decision we make and accepting personal liability is merely the first step to discovering freedom from the power of sin. Keep in mind, Satan wants to keep us enslaved to guilt, shame, and regret. He knows that if we hide in fear of judgment, we will never pursue Biblical repentance which requires us to change our ways. Instead, he wants us to remain quiet and not confess our sins, because he can maintain control over us if we never accept full responsibility for our actions.

Amber and I are many years removed from the aftermath of my adultery, but it all began with ownership and confession. One morning she said, "I had a bad dream about you last night. I dreamt you had an affair with _____!" Needless to say, I knew God had orchestrated that moment and I had a choice to make.

I could remain in hiding or confess my sins. Everything hung in the balance, but I had to accept complete responsibility for my actions and make amends for the foolish decisions I had made. Amber deserved to know the truth, and I needed to confess what I had done and humbly ask for her forgiveness.

In retrospect, my wife was incredibly gracious and merciful to keep our family together when my sins could have torn us apart. Today, when new opportunities present themselves to own the consequences of my actions, I do not act as if my sins are in the past. I fully accept them. It has also forced me to confess the affair to my daughters because I sinned against them as well. In turn, it gave them the opportunity to choose whether they could forgive me, because they deserved to know the truth and what impact it had on our marriage. In the end, God brought our family closer together because my girls now understand that He can restore what once was broken when we own the consequences of our actions.

Application

1. What does accepting full responsibility look like when you sin?
2. How has owning your sins helped you reconcile with your spouse?
3. Which sins of your past have you not fully owned that you need to remedy once and for all?
4. Think of a time when your spouse has accepted full responsibility for sinning against you? How has that inspired you to do likewise?

Reflection

"When I was a child, I spoke like a child, I thought like a child, I reasoned like a child. When I became a man, I gave up childish ways."

— 1 Corinthians 13:11 —

Day 37 – Attraction

I will unconditionally desire you.

"You are altogether beautiful, my love; there is no flaw in you."
— Song of Solomon 4:7 —

Physical appearance can be a sensitive issue, especially in marriage. The longer we are married, the easier it is to become unmotivated to eat right and stay in shape. Our bodies begin to show signs of wear, metabolism slows down, and busyness becomes hard to overcome. It is inevitable for most couples, though there are some who manage to maintain a more healthy lifestyle after getting married. However, most of us are apt to trend downward after our wedding because how we looked that day is arguably as good as it gets. That is why attraction is so critical. For when we do not look our best, we discover the depth of love our spouse has for us when we have gained more than a few pounds and cannot seem to lose it no matter how hard we try.

Frustration can wreak havoc on our self-esteem if we look in the mirror with disgust. For example, negative thoughts can impact our psyche and create marital problems. In turn, we must genuinely love our spouse and remind them of our continual attraction. Keep in mind, perfection is not literal but figurative as Song of Solomon 4:7 teaches. As such, we can remind our spouse that we desire them now more than ever because of who they are. We must also affirm them to combat fear and doubt so they know they are perfect for us. Undoubtedly, we have the power to overcome Satan's lies by speaking blessings to our spouse, but we must do so with sincere kindness and gentleness so our love may be received in their heart, mind, and soul forever.

After five pregnancies, it goes without saying that Amber has gone through a lot in 23-years of marriage. Her body has endured so much, yet I can say with full confidence that she is far more beautiful today than the day I married her, which is saying something because she was stunning in her wedding dress—pure elegance! I only wish she could see herself as I see her because she is gorgeous.

What I love about Song of Solomon 4:7 is that Solomon does not infer that his wife is actually perfect like God. What he conveys is that she is flawless in his eyes. That speaks to the heart of how I view my wife. Is she the same size as when I married her? No. Do I care one iota? Absolutely not! If anything, she is far more precious to me because of all we have endured together overcoming marital obstacles and raising four daughters. A marriage which is built solely on physical attraction is destined to fail because "charm is deceptive and beauty is fleeting" (Proverbs 31:30). It took time for me to understand the truth of that verse, but God has shown me that pursuing my wife mentally, emotionally, and spiritually is the key to lasting attraction in marriage.

Application

1. What first attracted you to your spouse during the dating years?
2. How can you reaffirm your attraction to your spouse each day?
3. Why is continual attraction so critical to a healthy marriage?
4. How has time made you appreciate your spouse more than the day you were married?

Reflection

"Let him kiss me with the kisses of his mouth! For your love is better than wine; your anointing oils are fragrant; your name is oil poured out; therefore virgins love you. Draw me after you; let us run."

— *Song of Solomon 1:2–4* —

Day 38 – Revival

I will invest in strengthening our marriage.

> *"My beloved speaks and says to me: 'Arise, my love, my beautiful one, and come away, for behold, the winter is past; the rain is over and gone. The flowers appear on the earth, the time of singing has come, and the voice of the turtledove is heard in our land.'"*
>
> — Song of Solomon 2:10–12 —

Godly marriages require time, energy, and resources to be successful. None of us just wake up in the morning and have a perfect marriage. We must work hard to achieve a godly marriage, and that requires intentionality to keep the fire burning. Every marriage needs a tune-up from time to time. Busyness often enslaves us to a hamster's wheel whereby we work through our daily obligations and reach a point of exhaustion. What we need is a break from the monotony—something out of the ordinary and spontaneous to let our spouse know we are not content remaining disinterested in each other.

There are a number of ways to spend quality time together but not every endeavor will meet our spouse's needs. We must be attentive and pay attention to what they enjoy to plan something special for them (which may require hiring a babysitter and scheduling a date night). We might even consider attending a marriage conference to grow closer spiritually. Whatever we decide, our plans must be selflessly motivated to ensure our spouse knows we have their best interest in mind, not ours. For if we love our spouse, we will do whatever it takes to let them know that aside from God, they are our top priority. Intentionality is crucial to guard against a stagnant marriage. It requires a continual investment of time and energy to keep the enemy at bay as we love our spouse sacrificially.

Early in our marriage, Amber and I attended Family Life's "Weekend To Remember" marriage conference. Our best friends lived near the facility so they offered to host us for the event. Keep in mind, the conference is known for making couples sit knee-to-knee and talk through questions to promote intimacy, but it can also create tension as well. When our friends picked us up the first night, we were quarreling and silence filled the air. We did not know what we had gotten ourselves into, but our friends just smiled and led us to their guest room. When we walked in, candles were lit, soft music was playing, and a charcuterie board and bottle of wine sat on the bed. In an instant, all the tension melted away. Our friends had attended the conference before and knew what to expect. They made sure our marriage experienced what it needed in order to survive the weekend and keep revival burning in our newlywed hearts. We laugh about it today, but that weekend is a precious memory we treasure because it taught us so much.

Application

1. How do you typically invest in strengthening your marriage?
2. Do you know what your spouse enjoys if you were to plan a special date with their interests in mind? Why or why not?
3. How have you fallen into monotony by not investing time, energy, and resources strengthening your marriage?

Reflection

"Create in me a clean heart, O God, and renew a right spirit within me. Restore to me the joy of your salvation and uphold me with a willing spirit."

— *Psalm 51:10,12* —

Day 39 – Intimacy

I will respect your sexual boundaries.

"Do not deprive one another, except perhaps by agreement for a limited time, that you may devote yourselves to prayer; but then come together so that Satan may not tempt you because of your lack of self-control."

— 1 Corinthians 7:5 —

Sexual intimacy is one of Satan's favorite areas of marriage to attack. He knows that men and women are wired differently, so it is easy for Him to create conflict in the bedroom. We have unique differences which dictate how we prefer to be desired, and those may or may not come to fruition based upon our mood, preference, or health. For example, there are certain times of the month when intimacy cannot happen. How then do we avoid the dangers of expectation and disappointment to find unity in sexual intimacy? It all begins with open communication and mutual respect. We cannot know what our spouse desires if we are not asking good questions, listening to understand, and applying pertinent feedback. It also does us no good to ask their opinion but disregard it in the heat of the moment.

The key is talking through sexual boundaries to avoid hurting our spouse mentally, emotionally, or physically. The last thing we want to do is make them feel as if we only care about ourselves. That is cancer to a marriage and will lead to bitterness and resentment. Instead, we are wise to talk through our likes and dislikes so we can better express love in a way that is positively received by our mate. For there may be trauma our spouse is harboring, and we must respect their feelings to ensure they feel safe and secure in our arms. Sexual intimacy is a gift from God we should treasure, and respecting our spouse's boundaries is the first step towards protecting their heart and mind to understand their thoughts and feelings much better.

Sex is not easy for many couples to talk about as Amber and I know well. It can feel awkward and embarrassing talking about what we each like and dislike. There are no right or wrong answers regarding what a couple agrees to enjoy in the privacy of their bedroom. God simply expects us to keep our marriage bed pure and undefiled. As such, we are to remain monogamous and avoid sexual idolatry so we are not tempted to seek satisfaction elsewhere. Obviously, I regret the years I spent filling my head with pornography because it distorted my view of sex. It took almost losing my marriage to see how depraved I had become, but I am thankful God gave me fresh eyes to see the beauty of sex from His perspective. Culture aims to define what is sexually acceptable. However, God has a different point of view which hinges upon setting firm boundaries to keep our marriage bed pure. I am simply forever appreciative that Amber gave me a second chance to learn what true intimacy is all about and rediscover the beauty of sexual intimacy from a selfless and God-honoring perspective.

Application

1. What are your spouse's sexual boundaries? Do you know?
2. How have you allowed cultural norms to taint your view of sex?
3. Do you ever talk to your spouse about sexual intimacy? Why or why not?
4. How has Satan used expectations to plague your marital intimacy?

Reflection

"Whatever is true, whatever is honorable, whatever is just, whatever is pure, whatever is lovely, whatever is commendable, if there is any excellence, if there is anything worthy of praise, think about these things."

— *Philippians 4:8* —

Day 40 – Pleasure

I will put your desires before my own.

> "Husbands, love your wives as Christ loved the church and gave himself up for her."
>
> — Ephesians 5:25 —

Once we have established sexual boundaries with our spouse, fulfilling their desires becomes our next priority. Sex is unique to a marital relationship because God intended it for procreation but pleasure as well. He blessed us with sex so we could enjoy the beauty of His creation and designed us to fit together by providing gifts of attraction, desire, arousal, and climax. Sexual intimacy was meant to be enjoyed in the strict confines of monogamous marriage, reserved for those who make a life-long covenant to love one another exclusively. That is why premarital sex is so devastating because a spiritual union is breached when we satisfy our fleshly desires immorally.

The key to reaching intimate satisfaction is by prioritizing our loved one's desires above our own. When we do, we experience joy because we are given the privilege of meeting their wishes in a way which is solely our responsibility. It is the epitome of dying to self and loving our spouse sacrificially. Marriage works best when we are reciprocating preferential treatment to each other, but that is not always the case. At times, our spouse may selfishly prioritize themself. However, it should not deter us from actively seeking to understand what our spouse enjoys and trying to fulfill their desires in a way where both are satisfied and sexual boundaries are honored and respected.

Pornography completely distorted my understanding of what sex is all about. I was focused on myself, so giving pleasure was nothing more than a manipulation tool to get what I wanted. I failed to see how sick and depraved I had become assuming that the images I looked at had any resemblance to godly, sacrificial love. That is the ultimate lie of lust, though, for it made me think that my wife's desires were identical to the fake portrayal of sex I believed was normal.

It was not until I learned how to please my wife for no other reason than to love her that my perspective changed. Sex was no longer an expectation but a privilege to love Amber in a way that no one else could. I have a newfound appreciation for the privilege of lying next to my wife and simply holding her. I am also far more sensitive to when she is not in the mood for whatever reason. She is precious to me, so it can be difficult to exude self-control at times when I desire her. However, I never want her to feel as if she cannot trust me. Rather, I want her to know that my one and only sexual desire is to please her, first and foremost, which is contingent upon me being humble and attentive to her needs. My goal is to prioritize her desires above my own because that is sacrificial love.

Application

1. What does your spouse intimately desire that you prioritize?
2. Why is manipulation so dangerous in sexual intimacy?
3. How can you meet your spouse's desires, first and foremost, when you agree to be sexually intimate?
4. How does your spouse feel when you selflessly meet their desires?

Reflection

*"You have captivated my heart, my sister, my bride;
you have captivated my heart with one glance of your eyes,
with one jewel of your necklace."*

— Song of Solomon 4:9 —

Day 41 – Companionship

I will celebrate life's joys with you.

"You make known to me the path of life; in your presence there is fullness of joy; at your right hand are pleasures forevermore."

— Psalm 16:11 —

We all long for happiness but having someone to share life's joys with is a precious gift. Waking up each morning and knowing our spouse is always by our side is comforting. It reminds us that we are never alone, for God has given us someone to share every precious moment. There are many reasons to celebrate during the year: anniversaries, holidays, and birthdays. The list is never-ending, yet nothing compares to sharing life experiences with the one we love most. It is difficult to put into words what it means to look back on all our seasons of life and know that our beloved was with us every step of the way. It is truly the epitome of what marriage is all about—two hearts coming together as one and discovering true joy and happiness.

Although marriage is a blessing, it can be difficult as well. When two sinful people get married, they are bound to disagree and have conflict. Nevertheless, the blessings of a hug, kiss, or smile from our spouse is enough to praise God no matter which trials we may face. We live in a fallen world. Pain and suffering are a part of life and hardships can steal our joy if we allow. That is why we must take the good with the bad and praise the Lord in the storm because pain and suffering provide context to our moments of happiness. Ultimately, it comes down to our attitude, because perspective forces us to find the silver-lining of God's grace and appreciate what He has done for us.

As previously mentioned, Amber and I are pretty frugal and pinch pennies where we can. We are not careless with our finances but save money which enables us to travel and sightsee as a family. We love to be with each other and one of our favorite memories was a road trip we made to the Grand Tetons, Yellowstone National Park, Mount Rushmore, Crazy Horse, Little Big Horn, and the Badlands National Park.

The best memory from that trip was driving through Custer State Park and coming across an enormous buffalo herd. At one point, we had buffalo grazing on all four sides of our old brown minivan. We joked that we fit right in, so we nicknamed our van "Tatanka," which means buffalo in Lakota. I also had a giant female elk lunge towards me in the parking lot of a grocery store outside Yellowstone. My family still finds that hilarious! Looking back, Amber and I treasure those memories because it was all about enjoying quality time as a family. Our girls mean the world to us, so anytime we get to see new things or experience new places, we try to include them and celebrate life's joys together.

Application

1. What are some of your favorite memories as a couple or family? What made those experiences such a joy to remember?
2. How can you prioritize making joyful memories with your spouse?
3. What about your spouse makes you feel thankful to God?
4. Who or what tends to steal joy from your marriage? How so?

Reflection

"You have turned for me my mourning into dancing; you have loosed my sackcloth and clothed me with gladness, that my glory may sing your praise and not be silent. O LORD my God, I will give thanks to you forever!"

— Psalm 30:11–12 —

Day 42 – Comfort

I will console you in your suffering.

> "Even though I walk through the valley of the shadow of death, I will fear no evil, for you are with me; your rod and your staff, they comfort me."
>
> — Psalm 23:4 —

There is no harder pill to swallow than watching your spouse suffer and knowing there is nothing you can do to stop it. Pain is a part of life that we cannot prevent, though we wish we could. It is simply a byproduct of living in a fallen world plagued by tragedy, disease, and famine (just to name a few). There is no end to the trials we face, yet there is hope and healing for those who trust in the Lord for salvation. Thankfully, we can be comforted knowing our spouse is by our side, speaking truth in love to our weary heart. Nothing compares to ministering to our loved one when they are suffering, for God has called us to comfort one another in our hour of need.

Comfort can take on many forms from providing a shoulder to cry on, giving a warm embrace, or being used as an emotional sounding board. As our spouse's closest friend, we have the ability to carry their burdens and pray for them as they seek the Lord's deliverance. We are not their personal Holy Spirit by any means, but we can encourage them to lay it all down at the foot of the cross to find rest (Matt. 11:28-30). Comfort is all about reminding our spouse who they are in Christ to protect them from spiritual warfare. Granted, it will not relieve their suffering, but it will point them to the only one who has the power and authority to heal their broken heart: Jesus Christ.

Losing loved ones is never easy. For instance, in the first 8-years of our marriage, we lost both my Mom and Amber's Dad to cancer. Time is extremely precious. So, when Amber lost one of her closest friends to leukemia at the age of thirty-seven, almost exactly one year after her Dad passed, it was almost too much for her to bear. It seemed as if God was calling home the ones she loved most which plunged her into a state of deep mourning and despair.

Death has been a common theme throughout our marriage. We've lost loved ones due to illness, my father most recently in January 2024, a child due to miscarriage, and a little girl who was tragically killed before we had the opportunity to adopt her. Yet despite all the tragedies we have endured, God has been faithful and brought forth beauty from ashes by using sorrow to strengthen our marriage. It has allowed us to appreciate family more and provided newfound perspective on the fragility of life, demonstrated by my heart attack in November 2022. Life will always bring trials, but we have learned the importance of always being there for one another. Thankfully, we know God is sovereign and that all things work together for good to those who trust Him for salvation.

Application

1. Give an example of a tragedy you have endured during the lifetime of your marriage. How did God help you get through it?
2. How has your spouse comforted you in seasons of great trial?
3. In what ways does your spouse prefer to be comforted? Why?
4. How can you comfort your spouse better? What needs to change?

Reflection

"He will wipe away every tear from their eyes, and death shall be no more, neither shall there be mourning, nor crying, nor pain anymore, for the former things have passed away."

— *Revelation 21:4* —

Day 43 – Patience

I will be patient with you.

"I, therefore, a prisoner for the Lord, urge you to walk in a manner worthy of the calling to which you have been called, with all humility and gentleness, with patience, bearing with one another in love, eager to maintain the unity of the Spirit in the bond of peace."

— Ephesians 4:1–3 —

Patience is a virtue, but it is really a fruit of the Spirit. Oftentimes, patience feels like a pearl of great prize, eluding us at every turn and remaining in hiding despite our best efforts to find it. No matter how hard we try, we cannot garner enough self-control to wait patiently and avoid frustration when life takes a hard turn. What we must realize is that patience is a gift from the Lord when we submit to His sovereign will. It is an asset in marriage because it forces us to stop living for ourselves and take our spouse's feelings into consideration. Conflict can arise when impatience is present, but it can be resolved as well when we choose to understand each other instead of complaining.

Being patient is all about the attitude of our heart. God wants us to let go of selfish tendencies and not place expectations on one another regarding how and when things get done. There is a time and place for accountability, such as helping a spouse who is always late to be punctual. However, patience elevates the need for understanding so we do not allow Satan to drive a wedge between us. No one longs to live with a spouse who cannot yield, bend, or consider compromise. Being held captive to expectations can destroy a marriage if we are not careful. Therefore, we must live patiently with our spouse to ensure we are not always sweating the details but being flexible with how they do things, for our way is not always best for everyone.

I cannot stand being late. Nothing gets under my skin more than walking into church on Sunday morning after the music has begun. Perhaps it was because my Dad made sure we were 15-minutes early to church growing up, but I have always made it a priority to be early for appointments or events.

Of course, God has a sense of humor and gave me a wife who struggles with time. Despite my best efforts to help her be more punctual, my lack of self-control has bubbled over on countless occasions when we have rolled into church late. It has certainly caused conflict through the years, but I have learned to put things in perspective and not sweat the details where time is not overly critical. Have I mastered the art of patience? No, but am I much better than I once was showing grace to Amber and being more considerate? Yes. If anything, her struggle with time is an opportunity for me to test my patience and live with her in a more gentle and understanding way.

Application

1. What has God taught you about being too rigid with time?
2. Are you more early or late to everything? How does that compare to your spouse?
3. What often causes impatience to overwhelm your heart and mind?
4. How have unmet expectations fueled impatience with your spouse and caused conflict in your marriage?

Reflection

"Be patient, therefore, brothers, until the coming of the Lord. See how the farmer waits for the precious fruit of the earth, being patient about it, until it receives the early and the late rains. You also, be patient. Establish your hearts, for the coming of the Lord is at hand."

— James 5:7–8 —

Day 44 – Grace

I will bless you when you least deserve it.

"Let us then with confidence draw near to the throne of grace, that we may receive mercy and find grace to help in time of need."

— Hebrews 4:16 —

Grace and mercy go hand-in-hand. The former gives us what we don't deserve while the latter chooses not to give us what we do deserve. They are both precious gifts from the Lord which reveal how much He loves us despite our sins against Him. It is a beautiful picture of His heart which goes to immeasurable lengths to bless us despite our failures. It also provides a blueprint for how we should treat our spouse when they are least unlovable and sin against us. The challenge is that we are human and demand justice. It does not seem fair to just pardon our spouse's offenses and move on like sins never occurred. We prefer that they wallow in guilt, shame, and regret for their foolish behavior. However, is that absolutely necessary?

Since grace is a gift, nothing should be expected in return when we bless our spouse. All we should be concerned about is reflecting God's heart and paying forward what He has freely given us with no strings attached. Keep in mind, we are no more deserving of His grace than our spouse so blessing them should be easier, not harder. The beauty of not holding our spouse's sins against them is that it allows us to forgive freely. It also reminds us that Jesus paid the ultimate price so we could die to our love of self. Satan does not want us to bless our spouse when they have sinned but to grow embittered towards them. As such, understanding the enemy's strategy gives us even more reason to continually show grace to our spouse.

Grace falls into the category of that which is easier said than done. It looks great on paper, but reality often proves otherwise. Adultery was the greatest test of grace and mercy our marriage has ever experienced. Amber certainly did not want to show me mercy. She wanted justice, but grace was a different story.

From the moment she picked up the phone and called our church for Biblical counseling, grace enveloped our marriage. She gave me the opportunity to fix what I had broken, but it was all dependent upon demonstrating that I was humble and repentant. Her act of mercy was not divorcing me or acting out in revenge when she easily could have. Instead, she chose to pay forward the grace of God she had received and gave me what I did not deserve: a second chance. The Lord enabled her to forgive me, and that act of sacrificial love and grace is the reason our marriage stands today. Truly, I do not deserve her kindness, but I am forever indebted to her for loving me despite my sins.

Application

1. From your perspective, what distinguishes grace from mercy?
2. How has God's grace been magnified in your marriage?
3. What tempts you to withhold grace from your spouse?
4. How has the love of God enabled you to forgive your spouse when they least deserved it?
5. How has your spouse shown grace which you did not deserve?

Reflection

"Blessed be the God and Father of our Lord Jesus Christ! According to his great mercy, he has caused us to be born again to a living hope through the resurrection of Jesus Christ from the dead."

— 1 Peter 1:3 —

Day 45 – Forgiveness

I will not hold your sins against you.

"Then Peter came up and said to him, 'Lord, how often will my brother sin against me, and I forgive him? As many as seven times?' Jesus said to him, 'I do not say to you seven times, but seventy-seven times.'"

— Matthew 18:21–22 —

Marital conflict is inevitable, for we are bound to say something which gets under our spouse's skin and creates tension. Most conflict is easily resolved by owing our transgressions and repenting of our sins. However, when we forgive but don't forget, we allow Satan to weaponize sin by building a stronghold of fear, doubt, and worry all around us. The enemy does not want us to forget the pain we felt when our spouse's sins came to light. He wants us to doubt their change and assume that their repentance was disingenuous. He would rather we play it safe and keep our memory active to ensure we are never fooled again. Yet, when we hold onto past sins, we prove how little we trust the Lord and His sanctifying work of change in our spouse.

God promises, **"I, I am he who blots out your transgressions for my own sake, and I will not remember your sins" (Isaiah 43:25).** Why then do we not hold to the same standard towards our spouse? If the Creator of the universe chose to not remember our sins, who are we to forever hold our spouse's failures against them? Keep in mind, we are not called to forget past sins as if they never happened. Rather, what God teaches us is that He will never hold us hostage to the past and hang a scarlet letter around our neck. If we are born-again, our identity is in Christ. Therefore, we can freely forgive our spouse and choose to not remember their sins just as God did for us as well.

The unique thing about forgiveness is that sometimes it is a daily exercise.

Amber would attest that it took years for her to not filter my present sins through the affair. Each time pride would rear its ugly head or my selfishness would take over, the scab in her mind would rip open again and take her back to the moment when my adultery first came to light. It was a vicious cycle which held her mind hostage for many years.

However, something extraordinary happened on our 20th wedding anniversary. Suddenly, it was as if she laid the hammer down for good and breathed a sigh of relief. Amber began sharing our story publicly and peace overwhelmed her. I can remember her sharing a testimony online about our milestone anniversary but actually revealing what we had been through. What struck me, though, was that she was ambiguous as to who was at fault in the adultery. She refused to place blame on me. Instead, she focused all her attention on what God had done in and through our marriage. It brought an element of finality to her heart because she chose to bury the hatchet and totally forgive once and for all.

Application

1. Why do you struggle forgetting your spouse's past sins?
2. How can you pay forward God's forgiveness to your spouse?
3. Are you holding onto your spouse's past sins? Why or why not?
4. How has your spouse's forgiveness been such a blessing to you?

Reflection

"For if you forgive others their trespasses, your heavenly Father will also forgive you, but if you do not forgive others their trespasses, neither will your Father forgive your trespasses."

— Matthew 6:14–15 —

Day 46 – Identity

I will affirm who you are in Christ.

"I have been crucified with Christ. It is no longer I who live, but Christ who lives in me. And the life I now live in the flesh I live by faith in the Son of God, who loved me and gave himself for me."

— Galatians 2:20 —

When we place faith in Jesus for salvation, our lives are no longer our own. We are rehabilitated, restored, and redeemed by the power of Christ's blood which cleanses us from all unrighteousness. The sin which once plagued us is removed and we are free to worship the King who secured our eternity in heaven. That is the testimony of every born-again Christian who confesses the name of Jesus as Lord and Savior. However, even though we may make a faith decision, it does not mean the enemy will stop attacking our minds with fear, doubt, and worry. He wants us to question the authenticity of our faith decision in Christ so we lose sight of our true identity.

As married couples, we have the ability to speak truth in love to our spouse in ways no one else can. We know them better than anyone and can discern when they are struggling to live out their faith in Jesus. Helping them see the power of God working in and through their life is a great privilege. It helps us support their efforts to live in obedience to Scripture and recognize the fruits of the Spirit which have taken root in their heart. God gave us no greater honor than to bless our spouse by preaching the Gospel to their heart and reminding them that they are more than conquerors through Christ who strengthens them. As such, it is a privilege to stand watch over our spouse in prayer and help guard them from the schemes of the enemy.

My wife is the strongest Christian I know. She is rock-solid in her faith and lives fully dependent on the Word of God for absolute truth. Nevertheless, there are times when the enemy plants seeds of doubt in her mind and tempts her to believe she is inadequate. Like most women, she is fully aware of her imperfections and tends to focus her attention on the areas she considers herself weak in.

From my perspective, Amber is the ultimate Proverbs 31 woman. She is smart, talented, proficient, and wise. She manages our home well, has raised godly children, and is as close to a flawless wife as any man could hope for. In all ways, she is perfect for me, but at times she can get down on herself when baited by Satan to calculate her self-worth based on what the culture deems important. It is in those moments when I remind her that her gentle and quiet spirit is the epitome of godliness. She is God's precious daughter, and that is the only identity which matters when all is said and done.

Application

1. Why is preaching the Gospel to your spouse's heart so critical to their mental, emotional, and spiritual health?
2. How can you better affirm your spouse's identity in Christ?
3. Which spiritual warfare tactics does Satan often use to attack your spouse's heart and mind? How so?
4. How have you failed to protect your spouse's mental, emotional, and spiritual health? What changes can you begin making?

Reflection

"Therefore, if anyone is in Christ, he is a new creation. The old has passed away; behold, the new has come."

— 2 Corinthians 5:17 —

Day 47 – Defense

I will guard you from persecution.

*"If the world hates you, know that it has hated me before it hated you.
If you were of the world, the world would love you as its own;
but because you are not of the world, but I chose you out
of the world, therefore the world hates you."*

— John 15:18–19 —

Persecution is real for those who proclaim Jesus as Lord and Savior. We live in a hostile world which refuses to believe the Gospel of salvation for sinners. Therefore, those who stand for righteousness will be targeted by the enemy and silenced in any way possible. When we embrace our identity in Christ, we are not expected to remain silent but stand for morality in a fallen world. Jesus did not suffer a criminal's death on our behalf only to watch us cower in fear to the enemy. He gave us new life so we could walk in victory over the powers of hell. Through Christ, we have confident reassurance that allows us to love those who hate us and bless those who persecute us (which can sometimes include those within the church as well).

Nevertheless, persecution is a tough pill to swallow. We can feel isolated when we follow God's straight and narrow path rather than conform to the pattern of this world. However, in marriage, we get to face the enemy as a unified front. Satan's ability to attack our blindside is diminished when we protect our spouse and guard their flank. Praying for one another and speaking truth over their heart and mind helps us shoulder their burdens and defend them when they are tired and weary. The benefits of becoming one flesh are put on full display when we face the enemy together, for hell has no power over us when we stop fighting each other and come together to defend our home against spiritual warfare and persecution.

Amber and I have faced the wrath of persecution for living out our faith in fear and trembling before the Lord (Phil. 2:12). We abide in Christ and follow His Word, so the Gospel is central to everything we say and do. Sometimes, our behavior convicts others because we live with intentionality and purpose. We have been verbally attacked by so-called friends and family, even in the church, which has brought us face-to-face with Jesus' promise, "If the world hates you, know that it has hated me before it hated you" (John 15:18). Persecution has been a tough pill to swallow, but God has continually assured us that He brought us together to protect one another. Amber and I are strong in faith separately, but we are even stronger together because we guard each other's back. When others hurl insults our way or attempt to tear us down for who we are, we lean even more into our faith because we know there is safety and security in the arms of Jesus and our love for one another.

Application

1. Which spiritual attacks is your spouse currently facing?
2. How has persecution strengthened your marital covenant?
3. Why is it so important to affirm your spouse with the promises of Scripture? What difference does it make?
4. How can you better protect your spouse from spiritual warfare?

Reflection

"Blessed are you when others revile you, persecute you, and utter all kinds of evil against you falsely on my account. Rejoice and be glad, for your reward is great in heaven, for so they persecuted the prophets who were before you."

— Matthew 5:11–12 —

Day 48 – Teamwork

I will share the workload in our home.

"By wisdom a house is built, and by understanding it is established; by knowledge the rooms are filled with all precious and pleasant riches."

— Proverbs 24:3–4 —

It is impossible to come together as a married couple and not work collaboratively to get things done around the house. No husband or wife should expect to do everything. Gone are the days when the husband went off to work and the wife stayed home to raise the kids and manage everything. Today, couples share the workload on many different fronts. The key is viewing household responsibilities as an opportunity to love and serve our spouse. Certain jobs are weekly, if not daily, because meals must be prepared, dishes washed, bathrooms cleaned, and laundry ran (just to name a few). We cannot ignore what needs to be done around the house. Otherwise, chaos will ensue.

It is also wise to avoid keeping score of who's doing what so we do not seek acknowledgement for our efforts. Expectations can easily lead to disappointment. Moreover, bitterness can develop when we fail to receive affirmation, so guarding against expectations is important to maintain marital health. Marriage rarely resembles a 50/50 ratio where both husband and wife equally share responsibilities. Our schedules may conflict or illness ensue. There are many reasons why we may not be able to share the workload at home, but that is why sacrificial love is so important. It guards our hearts from growing frustrated or angry towards our spouse and shifts our attention on working selflessly to honor Christ instead.

I thank the Lord that my mother raised me right. Growing up, she had me doing plenty of chores around the house from doing dishes, hanging laundry on the clothesline outside, helping prep dinner, and vacuuming. My father expected me to help cut the grass and wash the cars as well. That instilled a work ethic in me to not only do my share around the house but understand what it takes to manage a home properly.

Those lessons carry over for me today as Amber homeschools our girls while I handle cooking most of the meals. We share the role of cleaning and laundry, but the key for me is looking for unique opportunities where I can serve my wife sacrificially. I like to think about what is on her mental 'to-do' list and then attempt to alleviate some of her burdens. It lets her know that I am not only in tune with her train of thought but that I understand what weighs heavily on her mind. It also conveys that I will not take advantage of her by expecting her to do everything. She gives so much to our family on a daily basis and the least I can do is set aside my hobbies to serve her and our girls, first and foremost.

Application

1. How do you decide who does which chores in your home?
2. Do you serve your spouse expectantly or sacrificially? How so?
3. In what ways do you work well together as a couple?
4. How could you work better together as a team? In what areas has the enemy caused division in your marriage and home?

Reflection

"Whatever you do, work heartily, as for the Lord and not for men, knowing that from the Lord you will receive the inheritance as your reward. You are serving the Lord Christ."

— Colossians 3:23–24 —

Day 49 – Friendship

I will make you my closest confidante.

> *"A man of many companions may come to ruin,*
> *but there is a friend who sticks closer than a brother."*
>
> — Proverbs 18:24 —

Everyone longs to have a best friend to talk to, spend time with, and celebrate the joys of life. Having someone we can share our innermost thoughts and feelings with is a huge blessing, for it gives us a shoulder to cry on and a sounding board to seek counsel. God knew from the start of creation that it was not good for man to be alone, so He created Eve to be a companion for Adam so they would complete each other. Marriage is a blessing for many reasons, but friendship may be one of its most underappreciated. Knowing we can completely be ourselves with no judgement involved is comforting. We do not need to wear a mask or hide who we are because our spouse accepts and loves us despite our shortcomings and insecurities.

Oftentimes, we lose sight of what a blessing it is to be married. When conflicts arise, it can be easy to question whether we are truly compatible together, especially if friction persists for a long period of time. However, love covers a multitude of sins, and we can show more grace, mercy, and forgiveness to our spouse than anyone else. No matter how unlovable they may be, we can refuse to walk away because we vowed to love them in good times and in bad. The Lord knew we needed companionship, so He stepped in and provided the perfect complement to meet our needs. As such, we should thank Him for not only giving us a best friend to share our lives with but providing our greatest friend who sticks close than a brother: Jesus Christ.

Recently, Amber and I eclipsed the 23-year anniversary mark which also signified that we have officially been married for half of our lives. I can hardly remember life without her because we are one flesh and each other's best friend. Knowing that she will never leave or forsake me is such a priceless gift. I can be myself with her and remain confident that she always has my best interest in mind when she offers me wise counsel.

My heart attack over two years ago was quite the wake-up call for us. In an instant, our lives changed dramatically. I remember sitting in the hospital waiting for surgery but not afraid to die. My only concern was leaving Amber a widow to raise our girls alone. In our marriage, we do everything together. We share the workload at home and are rarely ever separated. We could not be more unified in marriage, so either of us losing the other would be devastating. I could not imagine life without her and she feels the same, but that is the beauty of being husband and wife and each other's best friend. We are truly one flesh in Christ!

Application

1. Is your spouse your best friend? Why or why not?
2. How is friendship an underappreciated aspect of your marriage?
3. What makes your spouse's friendship so special? How is it unique from any other relationship?
4. How can you avoid taking your spouse's friendship for granted?

Reflection

"Faithful are the wounds of a friend; profuse are the kisses of an enemy. Oil and perfume make the heart glad, and the sweetness of a friend comes from his earnest counsel."

— Proverbs 27:6,9 —

Day 50 – Kindness

I will not use my words to harm you.

"Let all bitterness and wrath and anger and clamor and slander be put away from you, along with all malice. Be kind to one another, tenderhearted, forgiving one another, as God in Christ forgave you."

— Ephesians 4:31–32 —

In marriage, we say things that we regret all the time. Whether intentional or not, sometimes words cut deep and wound our loved ones without us knowing it. Other times, we use our words as a weapon to inflict harm. Both are extremely dangerous if left unresolved. The key is knowing how to tame our tongue and bless our mate rather than curse them. Of course, it is easier said than done because learning how to put a bit in our mouth and bridle our tongue is no small feat. It is one of the hardest disciplines we will ever learn. As a result, we must focus on being kind to our spouse in word and deed so they know how unconditionally loved and protected they are in our care.

Kindness can be shown in many ways. Words are merely a starting point, but the attitude of our heart is where the rubber meets the road. If our intent is to bless our spouse, we will be cautious regarding how we express love to ensure our words are not lost in translation. If our intent is to harm, we will likely throw all caution to the wind and react upon feelings regarding what is in our personal interest. We cannot forget that kindness is a fruit of the Spirit. It develops over time and helps us care for our spouse's heart. The more we look out for their best interest, the more God will bless our efforts to sow seeds of blessings in our home. The key is developing roots of kindness in our words and actions so they can flourish over time.

I would like to say that I do well affirming and encouraging my wife, but I have plenty of room to improve. I am proficient at blessing Amber with words of affirmation, but I can also speak unkindly without realizing it. For example, if we are in a disagreement, I might roll my eyes or cut her off mid-thought. My use of sarcasm can be off-putting as well, communicating a lack of interest in what she has to say and demeaning her opinion.

The challenge is that I have no intention of hurting her in any way, but I tend to speak before considering the impact my words might have on her psyche. It has forced me to evaluate how I communicate to my wife in an understanding way. Now, I allow her to express her thoughts before giving my opinion. Interruptions have decreased, though my eye rolls are a work-in-progress! Still, what I am most concerned with is not raising my voice but speaking to her with love and gentleness. Truly, my words of blessing must outweigh the moments when I fail to bridle my tongue. Otherwise, I will not only hurt my wife but inadvertently tear her down.

Application

1. Why is kindness one of the true hallmarks of a healthy marriage?
2. How have your words become lost in translation because kindness was lacking? What have you learned from those experiences?
3. In what ways do you speak kindly to your spouse?
4. How has your tongue sowed seeds of cursing in your home?

Reflection

"No human being can tame the tongue. It is a restless evil, full of deadly poison. With it we bless our Lord and Father, and with it we curse people who are made in the likeness of God."

— James 3:8–9 —

Day 51 – Support

I will care for you when you are sick.

*"I was hungry and you gave me food, I was thirsty and you gave me drink,
I was a stranger and you welcomed me, I was naked and you clothed me,
I was sick and you visited me, I was in prison and you came to me."*

— Matthew 25:35–36 —

We live in a fallen world where pain and suffering are imminent. Illness cannot be avoided no matter how hard we try. In turn, we must weather the storms of life and love our spouse when they cannot take care of themselves. Illness can be difficult to bear. On one hand, we struggle watching our beloved suffer in pain. It is a helpless feeling but also a stark reminder that the Lord gives and takes away if He so chooses, for all of creation is subject to His sovereign authority. On the other hand, God empowers us to step into the gap and minister to our spouse in real and tangible ways. Granted, our workload will increase as we take on increased responsibilities around the house, but we will have the honor and privilege of nursing our spouse back to health if we accept being their primary caregiver.

Sickness is often one of the primary tools God uses to humble us by elevating our spouse's needs above our own. It puts life into clear perspective, at least what really matters, and prioritizes health over material possessions. Oftentimes, we fail to see the blessings woven throughout seasons of illness, but God uses them to grab our attention and refocus our efforts toward ministry rather than living to please ourselves. Illness is inevitable but how we respond to trials is what matters because the attitude of our heart reveals whether we genuinely love our spouse or not. For if we vowed to serve them in sickness and in health on our wedding day, then we are held accountable by God to be their primary caregiver no matter what the future may hold.

Like most families, we have dealt with our share of health crises through the years. Whether it be our health or that of our girls, God has always watched over us and brought healing to our bodies. We have dealt with our share of emergencies as well. Seeing Amber lie unconscious on our bathroom floor in a pool of blood after her miscarriage was arguably our scariest moment. It is difficult to describe how helpless I felt watching an ambulance pull up to our home and a group of firemen rush through the door to tend to my wife. I remember having to calmly gather my three girls and take them to a friend's house while the ambulance quickly transported Amber to the hospital. All I could think about was being there with her, but I had to make sure my daughters were taken care of as well. Sometimes like takes unexpected turns. We certainly did not expect to lose a child, but it was all part of God's plan. He was with us through it all and I am forever grateful that my wife made a full recovery by the power of His Spirit.

Application

1. What does it mean to love your spouse in sickness and in health?
2. How has God strengthened your marriage due to health issues?
3. Give an example of a health scare your family endured. What did you learn about self-sacrifice during that season of trial?
4. How can you be more sensitive to your family's health concerns?

Reflection

"But a Samaritan, as he journeyed, came to where he was, and when he saw him, he had compassion. He went to him and bound up his wounds, pouring on oil and wine. Then he set him on his own animal and brought him to an inn and took care of him."

— Luke 10:33–34 —

Day 52 – Loyalty

I will love you till death do us part.

"Where you die I will die, and there will I be buried. May the LORD do so to me and more also if anything but death parts me from you."

— Ruth 1:17 —

Marriage is all about commitment. On our wedding day, we stood before God and pledged to love, honor, and cherish our spouse till death do us part. It was a covenant commitment—binding in nature to guard our hearts from throwing in the towel at the first sign of trial or conflict. Healthy marriages are steadfast in their devotion to God and His Word. Scripture has much to say about divorce and separating what the Lord has joined together. However, the enemy is determined to divide us from within and tempt us to give up. Therefore, we must stand guard at our heart's doorway and ensure we are committed to love our spouse like Jesus would.

Unfortunately, death is inevitable. We cannot escape it no matter how hard we try. At some point, we will stand before the judgement seat of Christ and give account for our lives. Thus, we are wise to build a testimony of full devotion to our spouse before we breathe our last. There is no greater joy than to physically, mentally, emotionally, and spiritually care for our spouse until they enter heaven's gate one day and see Jesus face-to-face. Physical death is not our end but merely a momentary pause until we are rejoined together for eternity. Nevertheless, until that day comes, we must remain committed to one another until the Lord calls us home.

It is sobering to think of death. It is not something we like to talk about because we are focused more on the here and now than eternity. Death brings finality to pain and sorrow on this side of heaven, but our bodies will be perfected in heaven one day. We will no longer experience suffering because all things will be made new again. Truly, we all long for the day when we will be united with Christ, and that includes being with our spouse for eternity if they are born-again.

More than anything, our focus as a married couple of four daughters is to finish well. We want our marriage to be the most valuable legacy we pass on to our girls and their families. We want them to know their parents were not perfect but strived hard to live in obedience to Scripture all the days of their lives together. I want nothing more than for my girls to emulate Amber as their role model for what a godly wife and mother looks like. I want them to know that God restored our marriage for our collective benefit and His glory. Most of all, I want them to see what sacrificial love looks like through the lens of our redemption story. By God grace, we fought hard for our marriage, and we are determined to finish strong till death do us part because we are forever one flesh in Christ.

Application

1. How would you define what it means to be loyal?
2. Why is loyalty critical to keeping your marriage safe and secure?
3. What would you miss most if God called your spouse home?
4. How can you divorce-proof your marriage till death do us part?

Reflection

"Therefore a man shall leave his father and his mother and hold fast to his wife, and the two shall become one flesh'? So they are no longer two but one flesh. What therefore God has joined together, let not man separate."

— Matthew 19:5–6 —

POSTFACE

Finishing Well

What a whirlwind this project has been! When I set out to create this resource, my goal was simple. I wanted to write an easy-to-read devotional that a couple could do together to ignite revival in their marital covenant. The challenge was looking at marriage from a fresh lens and focusing on wedding vows we often take for granted. I cannot begin to express what a joy it has been to compose this book, allowing me to reflect upon what my wife means to me in fifty-two different ways. It is not easy summarizing aspects of our commitment to one another in just a few paragraphs. Nevertheless, exposing my heart on each page has allowed me to humble myself as I consider how gracious and loving Amber has been to me throughout our marriage.

As I have shared throughout this book, we have had our share of trials to overcome, but God has been faithful through it all. Even when it seemed like the wheels had fallen off, He gave Amber the strength to give me a second chance. Words cannot express how thankful I am for the opportunity to learn from my poor decisions and make amends for damages I caused. It has allowed us to appreciate what we have that much more because we know how it feels to almost lose it. Our prayer is simply that others would learn from our struggles and make the necessary adjustments to safeguard their marriages as well. We see our ministry as a pay-it-forward opportunity to bless others, and we pray that married couples find hope in Jesus like we did.

When I think about what comes next after completing a devotional like this, 2 Timothy 4:7 comes to mind. We see the apostle Paul looking back and giving a final proclamation regarding all he had endured in his lifetime as he focused on eternity. **"I have fought the good fight,**

I have finished the race, I have kept the faith" (2 Timothy 4:7). What Paul learned was that finishing well was everything. It did not matter where he started but rather how he finished. That nugget of wisdom is incredibly powerful because it paints a clear picture for what a godly marriage is all about.

Like most men, I was pretty clueless when I got married. I certainly thought about myself, but time proved how foolish and naïve I was in many ways. I had a tremendous amount to learn to be a godly husband and father. Unfortunately, I took the long, hard road to get there. What the Lord taught me is that sanctification is a marathon, not a sprint. Each day presents new opportunities to step outside my comfort zone and humble myself, and marriage is often God's favorite crucible of sanctification to mold and refine my character. There are days when it feels like he uses a sledgehammer to break through the walls of my pride, but I have learned to embrace His discipline, not fight it.

Amber would wholeheartedly agree that I am far from perfect, but time has shown that I am perfectible by God's grace when I die to my love of self. This devotional has been a priceless opportunity to focus my mind on the truth of God's Word and glean wisdom on how to be a more godly husband. Moreover, I am continually reminded of how blessed I am to have such a godly wife. She is my perfect match, and I am thankful that she challenges me daily to be a more righteous man of God based on her example of sacrificial love.

For better or worse, God resurrected our marriage from death to life and gave us fresh perspective on what it means to fight for a godly marriage. We are a work-in-progress like everyone else, but the Lord continues to draw us closer together as we pursue Christ-likeness in every aspect of our lives. It has truly been the key to success for our marriage—dying to self each day and sacrificially loving each other like Jesus would. It does not mean we have reached the promised land yet, but we are committed to finishing well no matter the cost.

JourneyIntoTheWilderness.com

DISTANT FROM GOD
Why the Struggle to Pray is Real

Do you struggle with prayer? Many do. Praying is a common weakness in the church today. We assume everyone knows how to pray, but nothing could be further from the truth. Sadly, many of us walk away from prayer rather than drawing near to the Lord. We are unable to experience its full power because our insecurities, anxieties, and self-doubt hold us back.

"Distant From God: Why the Struggle to Pray is Real" is a 40-day devotional designed to address the importance of prayer, why we struggle to pray, and how we can build a deeper relationship with Jesus. Whether you are someone who doubts the power of prayer, or someone who is looking to deepen your spiritual life, this book will challenge and encourage you to lift your heart to God and grow in your understanding of prayer.

Target Audience: Men, Women, and Teens.

JourneyIntoTheWilderness.com

LORD, I'M TIRED
Gospel Truth for a Restless and Weary Soul

Why am I so overwhelmed by fear, doubt, and worry? How can I resist giving up when the storms of life tempt me to lose faith? What is God's plan and purpose for my life when it feels like the walls are closing in around me? Why do I feel so tired and helpless, crushed by the weight of pain and confusion?

"Lord, I'm Tired," unpacks twenty issues which consume our minds, directing our attention toward God's Word for answers to life's trials. Whether enslaved to sin or struggling to resist temptation, we can discover hope and healing in the absolute truth of holy Scripture which casts light into the darkness of our hearts. All we need is to focus our attention on Jesus Christ to find rest for our weary souls and discover the peace of God which surpasses all understanding (Phil. 4:7).

Target Audience: Men, Women, and Teens.

JourneyIntoTheWilderness.com

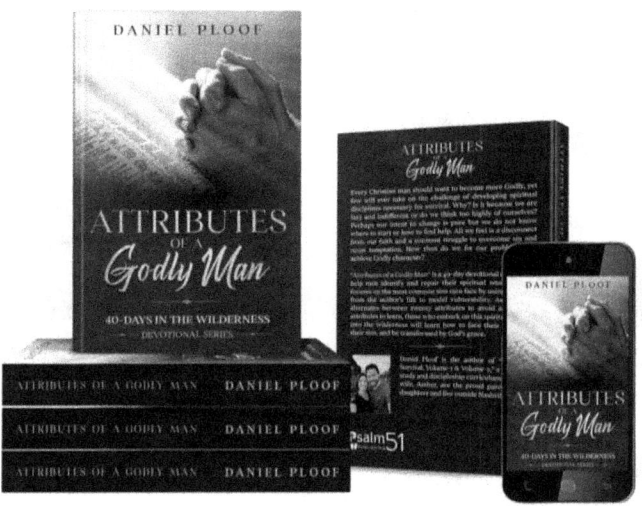

ATTRIBUTES OF A GODLY MAN

Every Christian man should want to become more Godly, yet few will ever take on the challenge of developing spiritual disciplines necessary for survival. Why? Is it because we are lazy and indifferent, or do we think too highly of ourselves? Perhaps our intent to change is pure but we do not know where to start or how to find help. All we feel is a disconnect from our faith and a constant struggle to overcome sin and resist temptation. How then do we fix our problems and achieve Godly character?

"**Attributes of a Godly Man**" is a 40-day devotional designed to help men identify and repair their spiritual weaknesses. It focuses on the most common sins men face daily by using examples from the author's life to model vulnerability. As each day alternates between twenty attributes to avoid and twenty attributes to learn, those who embark on this spiritual journey into the wilderness will learn how to face their fears, own their sins, and be transformed by God's grace.

Target Audience: Men, Women, and Teens.

JourneyIntoTheWilderness.com

WILDERNESS SURVIVAL
Volume-1 & Volume-2

Men's Bible Study / Discipleship Curriculum

Embark on a journey of survival training deep in the spiritual wilderness of isolation where few men dare to venture. Explore forty personal issues every man deals with in his life and marriage. Embrace the ultimate accountability challenge to become the man, husband, and father God calls you to be by transforming your life and changing your behavior.

"**Wilderness Survival**" is all about building Godly spiritual disciplines and surrendering to God's authority by examining your heart and filtering it through the absolute truth of His Word. The more you learn to guard your mind, the greater chance you will have of surviving the wilderness seasons of life and marriage, restoring the joy of your salvation, and defeating the enemy once and for all.

Target Audience: Men in relationships; preparatory for singles.

ABOUT THE AUTHOR

Daniel Ploof is the author of several Christian Living books, Bible studies, and devotionals including: **"Distant From God: Why the Struggle to Pray is Real," "Lord, I'm Tired: Gospel Truth for a Restless and Weary Soul," "Attributes of a Godly Man,"** and **"Wilderness Survival, Vol-1 & Vol-2."**

He is also the founder of **"Wilderness Survival Training,"** a resource platform designed to help Christian men and women find wisdom and discernment in God's Word. For more information and access to reflections, devotionals, and discipleship resources, please visit: **https://www.journeyintothewilderness.com**.

Daniel has been married to the love of his life and best friend, Amber, for over twenty-three years. They live outside Nashville, TN, and are the proud parents of four amazing daughters who are their greatest treasures this side of heaven.